CLASSROOM DIY

Setting up the classroom is a fundamental part of a teacher's job, as a well-planned, aesthetically pleasing environment encourages children to learn and helps with classroom management. Knowing how to create this environment is not instinctive and teachers are given little guidance, yet are expected to create a stimulating environment that is conducive to learning. The task can often be daunting and time-consuming, and teachers don't know where to begin.

Classroom DIY provides teachers with the answer to these problems. A practical, step-by-step guide, written from first-hand experience, this book will enable any primary teacher to make a spectacular job of setting up their room using any materials they have available. Guiding teachers through the process of setting up their space from planning to practice, this book includes advice on:

- Laying out the room: what furniture to use and where best to position it
- Organising areas for specific subjects, including maths, literacy, science and humanities
- How to create an inspiring classroom on a budget: recycling items for use in the classroom and the homemade approach
- How the learning environment can inspire and motivate pupils to learn, taking into account multiple intelligences and routines
- Meeting the expectations of senior management teams.

With 'teachers' tales' from a range of individuals in different schools and case studies illustrating solutions to teachers' specific problems with their classrooms, this book is a must-have for all newly qualified and practising teachers looking to inspire their pupils to learn through their classroom environment.

Maija Leimanis-Wyatt taught in a large, ethnically diverse north London primary school for six years and was appointed to the senior management team in her final two years. She is now living in New York City where she has taught at an international school.

CLASSROOM DIY

A practical step-by-step guide to setting up a creative learning environment

Maija Leimanis-Wyatt
Illustrated by Adam King

Routledge
Taylor & Francis Group

LONDON AND NEW YORK

First published 2010
by Routledge
2 Park Square, Milton Park, Abingdon, Oxon OX14 4RN

Simultaneously published in the USA and Canada
by Routledge
270 Madison Avenue, New York, NY 10016

Routledge is an imprint of the Taylor & Francis Group, an informa business

Typeset in Helvetica Neue by
Florence Production Ltd, Stoodleigh, Devon
Printed and bound in Great Britain by
The MPG Books Group

British Library Cataloguing in Publication Data
A catalogue record for this book is available from the British Library

Library of Congress Cataloging in Publication Data
Leimanis-Wyatt, Maija.
  Classroom DIY: a practical step-by-step guide to setting up a creative learning
  environment/Maija Leimanis-Wyatt; illustrated by Adam King.
      p. cm.
  1. Teaching – Aids and devices.   2. Creative teaching.   3. Classroom environment.
  I. Title.
  LB1044.88.L45 2010
  371.33 – dc22   2009024211

ISBN 10: 0–415–45877–3 (pbk)
ISBN 10: 0–203–86336–4 (ebk)

ISBN 13: 978–0–415–45877–1 (pbk)
ISBN 13: 978–0–203–86336–7 (ebk)

CONTENTS

Check before assembling

ACKNOWLEDGEMENTS

There are many family, friends and colleagues, without whom, this book would not have been started or finished.

My greatest thanks goes to my sister, Aleks, who made me believe that I had a skill worth sharing with other teachers and encouraged me to take on this project. Her remarkable skills as an editor, her unwavering focus and clarity of vision of the end goal helped me to recognise and develop a style of writing that would appeal to my fellow professionals. I will be forever grateful for her endless patience throughout my writing process and for her true dedication to this book. Thanks also to her team at *Dragonfly Communications* for their advice along the way.

I deeply thank my dear friend and once colleague Anna Archer. She is one of the most talented teachers I have ever had the pleasure of working with. This book would be half complete without her valuable input and willingness to share her wonderful creativity.

I wish to thank the following people and schools, without whose help illustration and photography would not have been possible:

My good friend and cartoonist extraordinaire, Adam King, for capturing the essence of this book with his unique style of funny illustrations; my photographer friend, Otto Inman who without hesitation found time to take on the random project of photographing pieces of classroom furniture; and Brian Walters for his retouching skills. Also: The Dwight School, New York; Earlsfield Primary School, Wandsworth; and Wessex Primary School, Maidenhead for allowing 'no frills' photography.

Thank you to my two former head teachers at Braincroft Primary School, London: Joan Richards and Chris Jones for always seeing my potential and commending my creativity as a teacher; and to Elaine Natalicchi, Dean of Timothy House, The Dwight School, New York for her continued support. Also, thanks to my colleagues who talked about their experiences and trialled my ideas.

I lovingly thank all of my family members and friends for unconditional encouragement and support, especially:

My wonderful husband, Steve, for believing in me and for enduring hours at the playground with our toddler to give me valuable child-free writing time; my Mum and Dad for pestering me to 'just get it written' and for helping out with child care wherever possible; and my friend, Ruth, for hatching a babysitting plan when deadlines were approaching.

Lastly, I thank my two children, Livija and Luke, for inspiring me to achieve my aspiration.

PART 1

Getting started

INTRODUCTION

A rude awakening

I began my first job as a newly qualified teacher raring to go. Of course I was thrilled about having a group of eager young minds to inspire, but what really excited me was the prospect of finally having my own classroom to set up just as I'd always pictured. The Arnold Schwarzenegger movie from the 1990s, *Kindergarten Cop*, is what springs to mind – brightly coloured, kid-friendly furniture, cushions galore, eye-catching wall displays and endless inspiring resources carefully positioned around the spacious classroom. No longer a student working in another teacher's room, I couldn't wait to have a place of my own to nurture.

So when I naively ventured into my first classroom thinking I would find a blank canvas on which to create my interpretation of a good classroom, I couldn't have been further from the mark. I discovered that the classroom to be my home from home for the next ten months was an utter disaster. Not only had I been allocated the worst room in the school (which is saying something in an under-funded, challenging inner-city school) but also, the previous teacher had stripped it of anything that may have proved useful. The paint was peeling, the windows dirty and the furniture looked like odds and ends from a car boot sale.

Crooked display boards remained plastered in staples from years gone by and there wasn't so much as a clean surface in sight.

As I stood there, my excitement quickly turned to shock and then anxiety when the realisation hit home. I had planned to cover my display boards, arrange the furniture, possibly even look through resources and walk out of there a few hours later well on my way to being prepared for the first day of school. But, transforming this uninspiring space into a carefully laid out, stimulating environment for children seemed unmanageable.

So where should I go from here as I accepted the challenge that lay ahead?

Why bother?

As a teacher, your classroom is your domain. It's how people first see you – the first port of call for the children, other teachers and visitors. What you do with it says a lot about you, and it's hard not to feel that your competence is judged by how you set the classroom up. It conveys the message that you're organised or disorganised, that you're creative or not. A lot of pressure can exist. You want it to be ready on time and you want to look like you know what you're doing.

At university, we're filled with ideals about how our classrooms must be stimulating, yet calm; how children should feel welcomed and inspired, and experience a sense of ownership for their 'home from home'. We learn that the careful display of children's work should provoke thoughts and questions and the set-up of resources provide on-going opportunities for independent learning.

The reality is that you get into your classroom and after a while you stop trying. It's overwhelming, hard to get inspiration, and there's just too much to do. You're constantly trying to work out how your time is best spent because even if you stay until the caretaker is standing at your door shaking his keys, there still aren't enough hours in the day. Do you spend that time after school planning lessons and marking so that you're organised for the next day, or do you prepare a display? And it can't just be any old display; it must tick all the right boxes. Teaching assistants can be an invaluable help, but the design of the classroom and knowing what you want to achieve with display areas is still your responsibility.

Learn from my experience

I did get that classroom to a standard good enough to receive the children on the first day of school, but I learnt the hard way, making plenty of mistakes. With each new classroom, I refined my tricks and discovered short cuts until I produced this seamless, step-by-step process for putting together a really great classroom, not just aesthetically but practically.

What you will get from this guide

Follow this guide and you'll have the fast track to a stimulating and purposeful classroom.

In a nutshell, this guide will:

- give you a focused starting point and clear steps forward
- show you how to use the time you have allocated for classroom set-up effectively
- help you use the space and furniture in your room to its full potential
- assist you in creating an environment that encourages creative thinking, is conducive to learning and well-organised
- show you how to make an impact.

Chapter 1

THE BIG PICTURE

When faced with a room in disarray, full of unfamiliar items and furniture, it's hard to know where to begin. It's about acting smartly; the key is to find out what's available to you and then do everything you can to get it.

Teacher tales

Every teacher knows that if you're new, you should expect the least desirable room in the entire school. Karen, a teacher with 15 years' experience, describes the situation in her school: 'Before school breaks up for the summer, it's pretty tense. We all bid for a classroom for the coming school year, which involves begging to stay put or to move somewhere more favourable. Then there's the hounding, occasional bribery and downright pleading until it's settled. Inevitably, the new, unknown teacher gets lumbered with the room that we've all suffered and will never return to!'

Two steps forward, one step back

In my first year, setting up the classroom was a painstakingly laborious process that I would never wish anyone to replicate. Not knowing the school or staff, I did things the hard way, and only later did I find out vital information that could have saved me time at the outset.

Two full days were spent wasting precious time and energy shifting furniture across the room, only to realise it didn't fit in the place I had envisioned. Or, placing something where I later realised I shouldn't have, such as in front of a plug socket that would need to be easily accessible. I then spent a day organising books in cupboards, not to mention dragging in an off-cut of carpet to help make an inviting class library and even vigorously cleaning surfaces. As I was arranging my final chair, a teacher told me that she had been promised one of the bookcases. When the caretaker arrived to remove the bookcase, he condemned the carpet off-cut as a health and safety hazard before announcing that a pipe running across the top of one of the walls was being replaced and the wall re-plastered. Finally the year group leader told me that my large, carefully organised cupboard, with its uncluttered sections for textbooks, resources and documents had to store additional resources for the year group.

Resist from moving or placing anything on that first day of setting up. Follow the next three stages of classroom set-up. Tried and tested, they are guaranteed to save time, keep stress to a minimum and prove productive.

Gaining insider's knowledge

There is nothing more frustrating than not knowing. Schools don't always appear to have a well-known policy for the purchasing of resources and it can be hard to know what you can get. It often appears that the staff members who kick up a fuss and ask for things, get them, while the rest of us try to make do, not wanting to ask the school to spend money.

You are entitled to find out **what is available** to you and **how** and **where** to get it.

Where the power lies

It is a known fact that two of the most powerful people in a school are the caretaker and the school secretary. They both hold keys to important, often unknown places.

When it came to mounting children's work early in the school year, I chose the best paper I could find – slightly faded tones of greens and browns. I later discovered that had I been part of the smoking crew, which included one of the office staff, I would have been granted access to a secret stash of beautiful A4 coloured card that was kept safely under lock and key to avoid being 'wasted'.

I am certainly not advocating smoking, more that it's definitely worth sussing out the office staff. They can tell you about basic supplies that are available such as staples, pens, tape, whether you get your own stock at the start of the year, or whether supplies are kept somewhere central to share. You need to know what you'll receive for the children in terms of pencils, coloured markers, etc. and whether or not they will be replenished during the year. I have been known to treat felt-tip pens like gold dust, rationing their use, not knowing if that's the lot for the year.

Befriend the caretaker

Much like the secretary, the caretaker takes guard of areas you may never know exist around the school, such as stashes of discarded furniture. Once he's your friend, it will be easier to persuade him to put your jobs at the top of his to-do list.

Teacher tales

Dorothy, a music coordinator who has been teaching for 20 years: 'I once sought a comfy chair for my class library. After much perseverance I befriended the caretaker. It paid off. He showed me a run-down Portakabin around the back of the school full of old furniture. I was in my element – even though these items were the dregs of the school furniture, it was great to have a choice – nothing that a bit of draped material couldn't fix.'

Put yourself in-the-know

Below is a list of questions you may need to ask regarding resources and furniture. Find out whom to ask and do not be afraid to request an appointment to discuss them. This way you'll be sure to have your questions answered thoroughly and you won't feel like a pest trying to ask them whenever a spare minute arises.

If you don't ask, you don't get

Questions to ask: resources

- Who should I speak to regarding resources that can be ordered?
  The bursar, secretary, year group leader/key stage coordinator, individual subject co-ordinators?
- How do I go about ordering resources?
  Do I do it myself or place an order through the appropriate subject coordinator?
- Is there a budget for ordering additional books/resources?
  How does this work? Is it allocated per subject/year group?
- Can things be ordered from websites or just through teaching catalogues?
- If I want to order something myself, will the school reimburse me?

- Are all of the resources for my year group in my room or might another teacher have some?
- Is there a central resource area?
  Is there a system for taking from it?
- Do I receive a stock of stationery items at the beginning of the year and what does this include?
  Will it be replenished at any other times of the school year?
- Are there specific books/stationery that my class must use?
  Size of maths squares or width of lines in ruled pages?

Questions to ask: furniture

- Is all of the current furniture going to stay in my room?
  Sometimes another teacher has put a claim on something and it will later be moved.
- Can I get help with moving furniture in my room?
- Will I be receiving any new furniture?
- Is it possible to order any new furniture if I need it?
- Do I have the right number of desks already in the room?
- Where are extra desks and chairs stored?
- Can anything that's broken be fixed/replaced?
  Is there a system for this, such as a waiting list?

Questions to ask: general

- Is there anything I'm not allowed to put in my room/on the walls?
  There may be health and safety policies.
- Where can I find ladders? Is there anyone who can help me with difficult-to-reach projects?

> Having done your research, you can avoid that overwhelming feeling of searching through mystery boxes and cupboards. You will have gained an idea of what's around and what's available to you.

The bare bones of it

It's hard to see the wood for the trees

Resist the temptation to just get stuck-in. Your room is probably crammed full of desks, chairs, boxes and other stuff so it's pretty difficult from the off to experiment with moving furniture around. It can be frustrating when you can't move something because everything else is in the way. Or you waste time hauling furniture across the room only to discover it won't fit where you wanted it, or there's a radiator in the way that you hadn't noticed.

Sketch what you see

Try to look at your classroom as if it were without furniture. Look at the parameters of the room and draw a simple sketch of what you see. Use my sketched example of a classroom I once worked in to help you (see Room Sketch 1). Do not worry about being able to draw well or drawing to scale; it's not about spending hours with the ruler – the idea is to just get a good sense of the classroom space you have to work with.

It's important to notice things like where the radiators and plug sockets are. Are there any alcoves or permanent fixtures in the room? These are all things that will affect where you can put furniture. Map the position of:

- windows
- alcoves
- plug sockets
- doors
- whiteboards
- permanent fixtures
- radiators/heaters
- display boards
- sinks
- obstructing pipes.

Make copies of your sketch so that later when you're experimenting with layouts, you can compare one option with another; or laminate your sketch so you can use a dry-wipe marker. Then put this to one side for when you are ready to create your vision.

Teacher tales

Joanne, a Year 5 teacher, says: 'I'm a "do-er" and can't bear planning things. I like to get on with it and get it done. But this year, when I was moved to a new room I had a bad back and knew I couldn't risk lugging furniture from one place to another. I tried sketching how I wanted my room to look first and planning where everything would fit. I couldn't believe how much more straightforward the whole process was. It took me half the time it usually would.'

Room Sketch 1

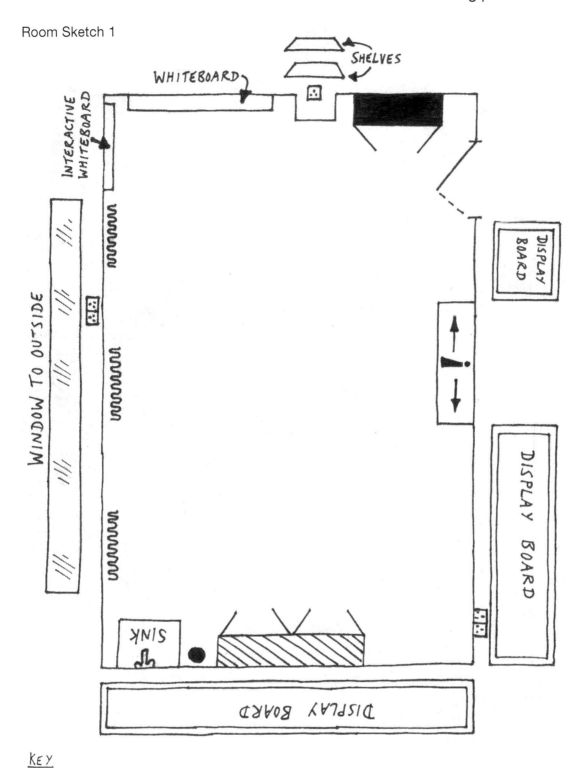

KEY

■ PERMANENT TALL FIXTURE

▨ PERMANENT MEDIUM-HEIGHT FIXTURE

←!→ DIFFICULT TO MOVE FURNITURE

wwwww RADIATOR

● PERMANENT PIPE OR PILLAR

⊞ PLUG SOCKET

Chapter 2

CREATING A VISION

How do you turn your blank canvas into a stimulating environment? By creating learning areas. When well planned and strategically positioned, learning areas make your classroom enticing, easy to manage and conducive to learning.

So what are 'learning areas'?

Learning area, activity centre, workstation and interest area are just some of the terms teachers use interchangeably to describe an area in the classroom assigned to an aspect of the curriculum.

Each area is a place where:

- a variety of activities, resources, equipment or artefacts reinforce and extend pupils' learning
- pupils are given the opportunity to work individually, in pairs or in a group
- pupils work independently, developing creativity and taking risks in a non-threatening environment
- the surrounding wall space is utilised to support and enhance the subject area. This could include the display of children's work, pupil voice, informative posters or interactive displays.

. . . and why use them?

A stimulating environment makes for a stimulated child. Educational psychologists have found that environment can have a big impact on children's learning. A classroom can either alienate or engage a child and much research shows that children who feel engaged in their classroom are more receptive.

Learning areas send out messages to pupils that the room is designed for them and the teacher wants them to enjoy learning. Pupils soon become aware that their efforts and work are valued. Because pupils use the areas independently, it gives them a sense of responsibility and ownership.

At their simplest, these areas are a perfect solution during a wet playtime or other times of day when there are minutes to spare or you want to offer a 'free choice' option to children.

If routines have been established they can aid learning, providing extension or reinforcement activities and promoting cross-curricular learning.

What is stopping you?

If you are not familiar with creating learning areas within your classroom, think about what has held you back.

- You don't think there is space – too many areas overcrowd the room.
- You believe that areas with activities aren't appropriate for the year group you teach.
- You are concerned the children will 'mess around' in the areas and that it will lead to unruly behaviour and a disorganised classroom.
- It will take too much time to set up and maintain the areas.
- You don't have enough or the right type of furniture to create areas.
- You think it encourages a way of working that is not structured enough for your teaching style.
- You believe that if you 'section' your room into areas, cross-curricular learning will be inhibited.

Teacher tales

'I hadn't considered creating learning areas until I saw Maija's classroom,' says Jocelyn, a Year 2 teacher. 'I thought they'd be too much work to set up and I didn't think young children would be able to use them properly. I couldn't have been more wrong. The children responded brilliantly, being creative and making connections they previously hadn't made. Plus the areas made my life so much easier. They provided activities when I needed to support or stretch a child and were so useful at wet play.'

Be realistic

In an ideal world, a classroom has space dedicated to each curriculum area. Of course, in reality no room can accommodate them all. If filling every square inch of your classroom walls is the only way to include each curriculum area, don't do it. There's a fine line between a stimulating environment and an overwhelming one that can confuse pupils and prevent them from concentrating.

Prioritise your needs

Listed are the possible areas to consider for your room with tips on where they could be positioned and their benefits. The list may be overwhelming. Forget about trying to cram everything in and pick the areas you think are most relevant to your year group and curriculum priorities. If space is a huge issue, look out for ideas that pop up later in the guide for making links between curriculum areas.

Learning area	Why have it?	Where should it go?
Class library	• emphasises the value of books and reading and fosters an appreciation of a range of literature • makes children feel that they are entering a special area • provides some seclusion, which minimises distraction when reading • the space can also be used for drama activities	• typically in a corner • a carpeted area • sectioned off by bookcases • don't rule out the centre of the room if you want to try something different
Literacy – writing	• places a special emphasis on writing and the writing process, encouraging time and care to be spent over it • enables children to pick up where they left off with the writing process	• an extension of the class library, backing on to a bookshelf; at a wall alongside the library; or inside the class library e.g. two sides library, one side writing table
Literacy – listening	• supports literacy and other subjects such as music and languages	• in the class library • on the floor by a wall with cushions

(handwritten notes) near to computer (old CD player) – headphones - split wires

Learning area	Why have it?	Where should it go?
		• put batteries in the CD/cassette player and this 'area' can be portable
Role play	• builds skills that can be applied to meaningful life activities • provides opportunity for children to play collaboratively and talk in role, developing important language skills • provides opportunity to explore class topics creatively • provides opportunity for links between all subjects	• typically in a corner • if short of space, look for a communal area to share with a colleague • if KS2 – could be based at a smaller area, such as a table
Maths	• opportunity to use maths equipment reinforces and consolidates learning • interactive display and visual aids promote thinking skills	• allocate quite a large area – it will house maths equipment, activities and games • could sit against a wall or comprise of several pieces of furniture to make an interesting arrangement that doubles as a workspace • don't place too close to children's seating or the whiteboard as it will be frequently accessed
Science	• supports development of practical investigative skills • provides opportunities for hands-on exploration	• amount of space you need to allocate will depend on how much equipment needs to be stored (science resources are often communally located) • consider positioning in front of a window – this could lend itself to elements of the curriculum such as 'Green Plants' and 'Light and Dark' • if sand and water provision is going to be a part of your classroom, position somewhere that facilitates manageable set-up and clean-up such as near a sink or a communal outdoor space (if available). Enable easy access all the way around and to and from this space
ICT	• supports and extends learning in all subjects • provides another medium for researching, recording and sharing information	• if your school uses laptops, you will not need a dedicated ICT area • remember to position any computer trolleys near a power outlet • if more than one PC, place together; if on trolleys, place back to back or create an 'L' shape

Learning area	Why have it?	Where should it go?
		• you are likely to need one computer near the interactive whiteboard • depending on the number of computers, consider placing one in the writing area • position so that the screens cannot distract others from working
Humanities (History, Geography, Citizenship, R.E.)	• encourages cross-curricular links • lends itself well to visual display and the display of artefacts to consolidate and extend learning • promotes chronological understanding through visual display • consolidates and extends geographical knowledge through visual display • encourages awareness of values and viewpoints of self and others • encourages development of enquiry skills	• at least one of these subjects is usually a key focus in the classroom, so allocate a large portion of wall space anywhere in the room • there is no need to create an area for each of these subjects – the focus of the space could be changed as necessary or one area could incorporate all subjects
Music	• conveys music as an equally important subject • provides an outlet for self-expression	• ideally, create space somewhere in the room for storage and display of instruments from different cultures • if space is lacking, store instruments in a container and link as and when appropriate to other curriculum areas
Art	• conveys art as an equally important subject • lends itself well to display – an opportunity to add variation and colour to the room • provides an outlet for self-expression	• if fortunate enough to have a sink in the room, base the art area around it • if no sink and children use one in a central area, position the art area reasonably close to the door to avoid too much traffic • if this area is to hold everyday stationery supplies as well as specific art equipment, it will need to be easily accessible
Design & Technology	• provides a place to display completed projects or to demonstrate the design process • provides plenty of practical opportunity to children to 'come and try'	• it's unlikely that you will have space for both an art and a D&T area, so these could be alternated

Other areas within the room	Why have it?	Where should it go?
Clear area surrounding whiteboard/interactive whiteboard	Various uses: • whole-class gathering area • space for children to present work • teaching space • space for floor work such as construction	• consider carpet/rug in this area • do not position children's seating too close to the whiteboard
Group work area	• enables children to work together in one space • enables teacher to work with a group • may not be needed if children's seating is arranged in clusters	• anywhere in the room where there is enough space • take into account noise that may be generated • this area does not have to be permanent. It can be created when needed by rearranging desks • the class library or a carpet area can be used for this purpose
Area for children's belongings	• if storage of children's books and personal items is not in desks, space in the classroom must be allocated for this so that children know where to locate and keep everyday books and belongings	• will depend on available furniture – must be easily accessible
Teacher's area	• aids organisation of your room and prevents teacher resources from getting mixed up with pupil resources	• an area near your desk and/or whiteboard to store supplies that you need frequently • if you don't have/want a teacher's desk, decide on one area in the room where you can conveniently store teacher's resources

Think inside the box

Now you should:

• have a realistic idea about the size and limitations of your room
• decide which learning areas you would like to include
• start to think about where you will position each area.

You should now be able to add to your sketch. Either sit in the room or remove yourself from it, whichever is likely to give you the most inspiration, and loosely mark learning areas on your sketch. If you think your sketch might start to look unclear or confusing, use a different coloured pen or lay an overhead transparency sheet over your room outline sketch for the marking of areas. See Room Sketch 2, showing how I planned out the learning areas in this classroom.

When positioning, you will need to consider:

- traffic flow
  Which areas will be accessed most by the children? Which will you, the teaching assistant and other support staff, need to access the most? Make sure that children's seating does not block access to these areas.
- health and safety
  The area near the door should allow for a clear, rapid exit. If children line up here, avoid things that could get knocked over. Children should not be able to be hidden from view anywhere in the room.
- the front and back of the room
  If children's seating faces the front of the room, would it be less distracting to have more active areas near the back?
- the positioning of areas in relation to the teacher's desk or place where the teacher is mainly stationed
  Can you see all the areas you need to be able to see when seated?
- quieter areas and noisier areas
  Consider potential noise levels and whether or not to separate quieter areas from more active areas.

The room in reality

This classroom of mine was not perfect, as no room is (see example room sketch 2). Although it annoyed me to make one or two sacrifices to my 'ideal room', once the school year was in full swing, I didn't even notice and I managed to make it work. If the layout of your room isn't working for you, there's no harm in re-thinking. Here is some of the reasoning behind my decisions for this specific room.

It seemed obvious where the **teacher's area** would go – the shelves were out of children's reach and the large, immovable cupboard easily housed all of my folders and resources for photocopying. I positioned my desk jutting out from the alcove next to the whiteboard, looking onto the gathering area. Somebody later told me that it would create negative Feng Shui to have my back to the door, but as it happened, I didn't actually sit at my desk very often anyway.

The **radiators** were an annoyance because they prevented me from putting furniture along one whole side of the room. I managed to squeeze a tall, narrow shelving unit between the sink and the radiator for art supplies. I had wanted an **art table** where individuals could sit for artistic inspiration but there was no room for it in the art area, so I had to think around this.

I found the solution in the **music area**, which consisted of a display table with space underneath where I stored instruments in plastic containers. This table alternated between music, art and also **D&T**. The windowsill above was deep and so became a good space for displaying D&T projects.

Room Sketch 2

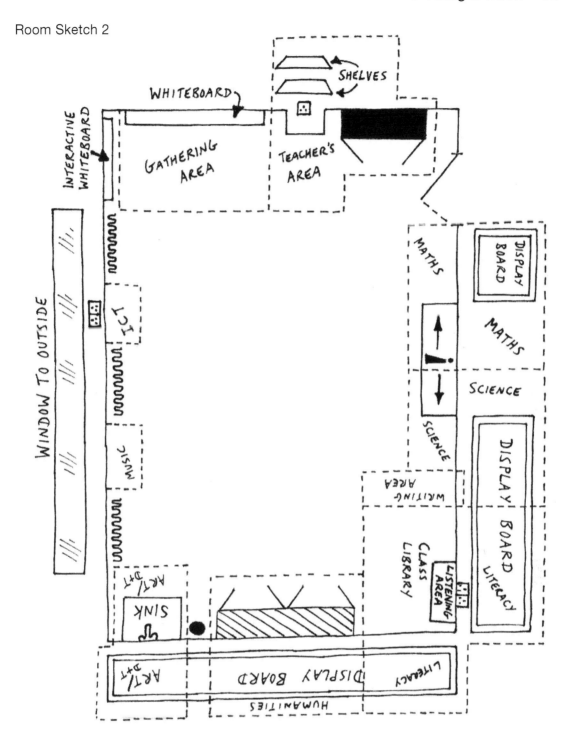

KEY

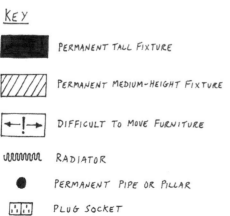

PERMANENT TALL FIXTURE

PERMANENT MEDIUM-HEIGHT FIXTURE

DIFFICULT TO MOVE FURNITURE

RADIATOR

PERMANENT PIPE OR PILLAR

PLUG SOCKET

The **ICT area** was initially a computer trolley that was later replaced by a table with two laptops on it. This provided flexibility and it often doubled up as an **additional writing area** or sometimes a **'time-out' table**.

It made sense to divide up the two long **display boards** in the room. I did this by using different coloured backing paper and borders. This also helped define the learning areas in front of the boards.

The large piece of furniture on the same side of the room as the classroom door was extremely hefty and so it had to stay put. It had several deep shelves and sliding doors, so this space was perfect to split between **maths** and **science** resources that I needed the children to be able to access independently. The surface was useful for interactive display and activities which extended onto the furniture I placed either side of this large piece. Ideally, I hadn't wanted the maths and science areas side by side because they would both be busy areas visually and in activity. However, this was the best option in terms of best use of furniture and available display space.

The rectangular **class library** space was created by bookcases jutting out from the walls, with the **writing area** consisting of a table set against the back of two of these bookcases. I wanted the writing area close to the class library and I liked this arrangement because it created a nook in which children could sit, facing away from the main area of the room. Also, placing the writing area here enabled me to give a coherent look to literacy display.

When planning your classroom, some areas will be immediately apparent, such as the most suitable place for the class library or positioning the art area near the sink. Others may not be so easy to decide and you may need to have a better idea of the furniture you have to work with before you can do this, so read on before revisiting your classroom sketch.

Furniture: the basics and where to put them

Having decided on the positions of the learning areas, the next task is to find pieces of furniture to create them. When it comes to our classrooms, there are no 'basics' in terms of furniture. It's simply what you've got, and other than desks and chairs, that could be anything. It isn't always obvious what to put where. You need to assess what you have and then use it to its best advantage.

The furniture you select and how you arrange it to create the areas can affect:

* the look and feel of the room
* the usability of the room
* the efficiency of the room.

Make a list

As a teacher, there's always a list to make, but don't labour over this one. Use this checklist to note the different types of furniture in your room and how much you have. Being aware of the types of furniture available to you will help you in deciding:

* whether you have room for all of your furniture
* whether you want to try to 'trade' for different pieces of furniture or gain additional pieces
* the best practical use for each piece.

Then, use the suggestions and the pictures of various types of furniture to help you.

Furniture checklist

Type of furniture	Number available	Notes
Bookcases:		
tall	☐	
medium	☐	
low (e.g. library box)	☐	
Deep shelving unit: medium	☐	
Closed shelving unit (cupboard):		
tall	☐	
medium	☐	
Unit of drawers:		
plastic trays	☐	
chest of drawers	☐	
Children's seating:		
individual desks	☐	
double desks	☐	
larger tables	☐	
Teacher's desk	☐	
Chairs:		
pupils' chairs	☐	
adult-sized chairs	☐	
other (e.g. easy chair)	☐	
Filing cabinet	☐	
Computer trolley	☐	
Book rack/stand:		
wire (attached to wall)	☐	
hanging pockets	☐	
free-standing	☐	
Free-standing whiteboard	☐	
Other:		

Large pieces of furniture

Medium-height bookcases are ideal for the class library so that all books, even those displayed on top, are within children's reach. Three would allow you to create a defined library area.

Low-level 'library boxes' are useful for storing picture books and other larger books such as non-fiction and reference books. Especially popular with key stage 1 because young children can remove books and put them back easily.

If your room has a book rack fixed to the wall, don't let that determine where you have your class library. You could ask for it to be moved, or use it for something else in its current location such as a display area for books/ newspapers you want to bring to pupils' attention. Or, children's work could be displayed in the rack if mounted on sturdy card. Wire bookracks can be used to hang things from or to hold book bags containing activities.

Units with deep shelves are useful for the science, maths and also the humanities area.

Shelves should be deep enough to house baskets, containers and tubs of resources and equipment. Pupils' workbooks and textbooks also store well in this type of unit.

Medium-height, deep units are most practical because children can access resources easily and the tops can be used for display. The simple attachment of a curtain is a clever way of hiding messy art supplies.

Tall units work well for your teacher resources and files. The lower shelves could be used for textbooks and workbooks. If you have a lockable cupboard, use it in the teacher's area for storing your personal belongings and teaching resources.

Not many classrooms have them, but a filing cabinet is a real luxury for keeping pupil assessments, portfolios and INSET/staff meeting material in order. Expandable files kept in a cupboard can work just as well.

Computer trolleys are still around in lots of our classrooms, but are quite cumbersome. If you use laptops, storage is much more versatile. You might want to dedicate a table as an ICT area where children can sit and work or it might be easier for children to take the laptops to their seat.

Units with pull-out trays are great for categorising resources, for example for maths and science. They are also useful for separating different types of paper. A popular use is for children's books and personal belongings, but if overstuffed, trays easily get trapped.

A free-standing, portable whiteboard is a versatile item, useful in the class library or gathering area. Some have storage space for big-books underneath.

Smaller items

Hanging pockets are handy for extra book storage anywhere in the room. Those with lots of pockets have multiple uses; each child can be allocated a pocket – this can hold his/her ticket from a borrowed book for example, or unfinished pieces of work, helping to prevent them from being misplaced. Pockets can also serve as a 'post box' for letters/homework sheets, etc., to be taken home.

Soft furnishings

Two carpet pieces or rugs are ideal – one to make the class library feel cosy and one to define a gathering area in front of the whiteboard or elsewhere in the room. Single carpet tiles/squares can be useful if the room has hard flooring; children take them to a floor area to use as workspace.

An interesting chair can add something special to a room and be inspirational. It can provide a special place for children to perform, present or become 'story-teller' for example. Use cushions, bean-bags or an armchair to furnish the class library, listening area and gathering area making them comfortable and inviting. Cushioned lap-trays are useful and usually viewed as a 'treat' when working in the class library or other floor areas.

Containers

A well-organised classroom demands a range of storage containers. See 'make-do and mend' for further ideas.

Magazine files are useful for class library resources that don't sit well on shelves such as magazines and newspapers. To avoid damage and wastage, paper in the writing, art and ICT areas should be stored in trays. Stand-alone trays work well for 'scrap' paper to re-use, homework 'in' trays, 'books to be marked' trays, etc. Stackable trays help keep paper organised on the teacher's desk. Try stacking five trays on your desk labelled with the five days of the school week. In the relevant tray, place books/sheets to be photocopied, sets of sheets to be handed out, etc. You will need larger containers, preferably with lids for storing resources such as musical instruments, construction materials, dressing-up clothes and props.

Using a desk organiser in the writing centre provides a ready supply of pens and pencils. Either a basket or a type of desk organiser is essential for items shared by a group of children at one time such as marker pens, coloured pencils, rulers, etc. The art area requires many pots and tubs.

Make-do and mend

If your school is lacking in storage containers, there are plenty of homemade alternatives.

Item	How to use it
Biscuit/cracker tins	Storage of maths or art equipment, writing area activities, paper supplies
Cereal boxes, crisp or biscuit tubes, yoghurt pots, plastic sweet jars, fizzy drink bottles cut in half, ice-cream cartons	Storage of maths or art equipment or stationery supplies
Roll-on deodorant plastic bottles	As a paint dispenser
Paper bags	Can be pinned to the wall in any area to hold activity cards
Shoe boxes	Storage of maths or art equipment, paper, CDs and tapes
Shoe organiser	Hanging pockets for storage of mental maths games/cards/resources
Wine boxes cut in half and covered	Storage of A4-sized books or magazines
Plastic sandwich bags of various sizes (zipped ones last longer)	Storage of cards and games

Add furniture to your sketch

Revisit your sketch and plot the contents of your room. Sketch and re-sketch furniture arrangements until you're satisfied that it will work. It will be trial and error and you probably won't actually know if some pieces of furniture will fit until you physically try it. The most important aspect of sketching is the planning process you will go through in getting to the point of deciding what should go where and why.

How to tackle a difficult room

Classroom set-up can be made particularly challenging if your room is not a perfect rectangle or square shape, but do not lose hope. Exceptionally large or small rooms pose a challenge, as do rooms with lots of windows, open-plan classrooms and rooms with high ceilings. Here are a few problem scenarios we commonly face, with some suggested solutions.

The problem . . .

'My classroom has windows along one length of it to the playground and glass along another to an internal corridor,' says Year 4 teacher, Pascale. 'There's just not enough wall space so this makes it difficult to create displays where I want them. I've tried to attach backing paper to the glass for displays, but after a while the paper gapes and it just looks shoddy.'

Solution ideas . . .

1   Try to get hold of some fairly large pieces of thin hardboard and then ask the caretaker to nail them to the back of drawer units, bookcases, etc. Cover the hardboard with backing paper – it will make for a neat display board, attached to a surface area. The same solution can be used in a classroom that has a folding door or an open-plan room where wall space is sparse.
2   Although backing paper is likely to gape or slide off glass, attaching it to the window surround may work better.
3   Another idea is to hang a covering from the ceiling in front of the glass, such as material, and then pin children's work to it.
4   Visit a garden centre to find vegetable netting or lattice that can sit/hang in front of a window and be used to attach children's work to. Since it is less solid than paper or material, it won't block as much light.
5   Make the most of a window by having the children create 'stained glass' artwork.

The problem . . .

'My room is large and unhomely,' says Year 1 teacher, Gary, 'and I know that I'm not filling the space in the way that I could. Also, it has high ceilings and so parts of the display boards are hard to reach. Not only is it difficult to climb up to change the displays, you can't even read the children's work when it's that high up.'

Solution ideas . . .

1   To make the room appear more decorated, use bold, rich colours for display.
2   Add soft furnishings – material pinned and draped or rouched across windows creates a homely look, as does a lamp on the teacher's desk or in the class library (if permitted due to health and safety). Also, cushions, beanbags and rugs pull a room in, and if there is space, an old sofa would add something special to a reading area.
3   If the display boards are huge, split them horizontally using the upper section for bold, visual displays, such as children's artwork, dioramas or models (for example, parts of

a flowering plant). If there is a lot of wall space above the boards, use it for permanent display such as signs and posters so that it doesn't have to be changed during the year. Use the lower part of the board for children's written work that needs to be seen up close.

4   To bring work on display to the children's level, hang string from the ceiling and attach work to it. If the ceiling is too high to reach, hang display from a washing line across the room.

5   With a large classroom, creating learning areas is a delight because you can place furniture in a way that juts out in order to separate them. In addition to a class library, perhaps there is room for an additional gathering area with a rug. Have fun and use large furniture boxes and/or material to create something exciting and possibly topic-linked like a cave or a rainforest.

The problem . . .

'My room is a portakabin and so is pretty small,' says Year 3 teacher, Kate. 'I don't have a lot of additional furniture because there isn't much space around the children's desks; this makes creating learning areas particularly challenging.'

Solution ideas . . .

1   Carefully consider which learning areas are priorities; don't try to include all subjects – they could be rotated. Do try to create a class library; this could double-up as a gathering area.

2   Opt to arrange children's desks in groups so they take up less space and even group some desks around the teacher's desk.

3   Shelves are a great solution to take the place of furniture that would stand against a wall. These can be placed at varying heights, some most definitely at the children's level. Use them for storage of resources or as a display surface. Store resources in hanging pockets, for example a shoe organiser that hangs from a nail or hook.

4   If there's not enough room to create separation between areas, contrasting colours of backing paper and borders on the wall helps separate areas visually. Also, clearly and attractively label displays as 'maths', 'science', etc. to prevent a busy room from looking too confusing to the eye. Remember to also utilise the space on the back of the door as well as the front of any cupboards.

5   Displays do not have to be restricted to the wall. Display work on large pieces of concertinaed cardboard that can be placed anywhere and moved around or removed if need be.

Arranging children's seating

The four most common seating configurations are no doubt familiar to you:

*   clusters of desks/tables to form groups of four, six or eight where children face one another
*   desks/tables aligned in rows facing the front of the room
*   desks/tables arranged in a U-shape/horseshoe/chevron
*   desks in pairs or tables that seat two.

Many teachers' books include seating configurations and although this one does not promise to show you anything you don't already know, the reasons why real teachers in real classrooms either love them or hate them may help you decide which could work for you in your classroom.

Clusters

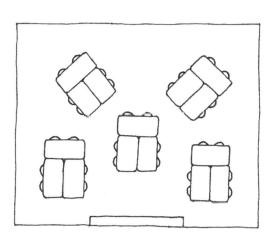

Teachers like this arrangement because:

- desks/tables seem to take up less room
- a good amount of space remains around the outer edges of the room to access learning areas
- it facilitates group collaboration and makes sharing resources and equipment easy
- it allows for easy traffic flow around the room for both teacher and pupils
- it is good for small group teaching, either mixed-ability or ability groups
- table groups can be named giving children a sense of community.

Teachers don't like this arrangement because:

- when teaching a whole-class lesson, some children may not be facing them
- children sometimes become competitive about table groups
- children are more likely to chat.

Rows facing the front of the room

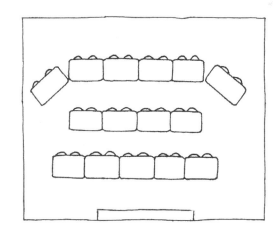

Teachers like this arrangement because:

- children all face the front of the room
- some children's attention to their individual work increases when no-one sits opposite them.

Teachers don't like this arrangement because:

- it is difficult to move around the room
- it is not easy for children to share equipment, so more supplies may be needed
- it is not conducive to group work unless children turn to face the row behind them. This works for discussion, but if written work is also necessary, there is little surface space
- some children are inevitably seated at the very back of the room and in the corners.

U-shape/horseshoe/chevron

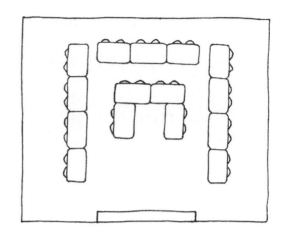

Teachers like this arrangement because:

*   each child can be easily seen
*   all children can see the board easily
*   it works well for whole-class discussions
*   it is easy to get around the room
*   it allows a large central space for role play and presenting
*   children can work in pairs.

Teachers don't like this arrangement because:

*   it takes up the entire classroom space and it is hard to get to outer learning areas
*   it is not easy for children to share equipment, so more supplies may be needed
*   children only have two other people close by to work with
*   the desks/tables get knocked out of position easily
*   it makes group work difficult.

Teacher tales

Deputy head teacher Debbie says: 'I once organised my Year 5 classroom with desks in a horseshoe, having promised the children an arrangement of their choice. I was reluctant because it wasn't conducive to group work and I told them it would only work if they could rearrange the desks for group activities. It took some practice but they did it successfully. It was a military operation of little furniture movers – we got it down to 20 seconds.'

Pairs or tables that seat two

Teachers like this arrangement because:

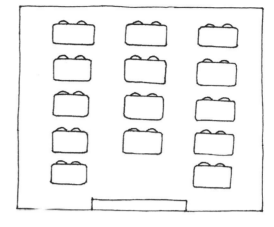

- children can work with a partner
- children face the front of the room
- some children concentrate better with fewer people sat around them.

Teachers don't like this arrangement because:

- children can only share equipment with one other person, so more supplies may be needed
- desks/tables must be accurately positioned and stay in these positions to allow for good traffic flow
- children often tire of being seated next to the same person.

Teacher tales

Abi, a Year 4 teacher recalls: 'Every time I feel enthused to try out a new desk arrangement, it goes like this – I lug furniture around the room, trying to fit it like a jigsaw puzzle. More often than not, what I had in mind doesn't quite fit as I hoped and I end up putting them back as they were.'

Experimenting with a new seating arrangement can be frustrating. Take your laminated room sketch and play around by drawing the outline of desks/tables. Alternatively, make a desk/table template roughly to scale; photocopy and cut out the number you need. Experiment by physically placing them on the page. This way, you won't pull a muscle.

Positioning the teacher's desk

How do you view your desk?

a   It's a base for everything; it's where I sit to observe children working, mark children's work, work one-to-one with children and keep my resources.
b   I rarely sit at it but use it to store my resources and personal items. It's a bit of a dumping ground.
c   It's somewhere to perch as I teach.

How you view your desk has an impact on where in the room you'll find it works best.

Placing your desk at the front of the room

- The whole class faces you and is clearly visible.
- It is useful to position yourself close to the whiteboard if this is main teaching area.
- You can sit at it to teach.

Placing your desk at the back of the room

- The children sometimes forget that you can see them and so you get a true reflection of behaviour.
- When working one-to-one with a child, others are less likely to be disturbed.
- If it's messy, children don't focus on it.

Placing your desk in a corner

- Creates your own area within the room.
- Feels more private for conferencing with individuals.

Teacher tales

Year 5 teacher, Hari, has an interesting take on using a teacher's desk: 'I don't want to waste any of my valuable space by using a desk for myself, so I happily got rid of my antiquated desk. It cast an authoritative spell on the climate. I use a filing cabinet to store class records and a tall cupboard for my teaching supplies.'

Make an initial decision about whether or not you want a desk and where to place it, but bear in mind that it may not be until your room is in practice that you discover where you really want it.

The skeleton of your room is now complete. It's time to get down to the nitty-gritty.

PART 2

Setting up

INTRODUCTION

The nitty-gritty – setting up learning areas

You've decided how many learning areas you want and can fit in your room. So what do you put in them? I have found the perfect learning area contains three things: storage space for the resources regularly used for that subject; a display on the wall and corresponding surface area with interactive questioning and items of interest, as well as available activities that reinforce or extend learning.

An example learning area – take a glimpse

It may seem obvious but often teachers miss the opportunity to bring all three things together and it is this combination that will make your classroom a creative learning environment that really works.

A good example of a missed opportunity is what my friend did with her Year 5 classroom. She had set up a geography display on a table with a globe and a pile of atlases. The wall behind was not a fixed display board but had room for posters and on it she had stuck a large 100-number square and some punctuation reminders. All useful and interesting but it just wasn't clear what was going on here. The area wasn't defined as anything in particular. We moved the posters elsewhere and replaced them with a world map (as permanent display). To link to the current unit on Kenya we added the question, *Can you find Kenya on this map?* We put up posters of Kenya with the questions, *What do you think the climate is like in this country?* and *What are the clues?* On the table we put some pictures of animals sculpted in wood and a typical African Calabash (bowl) with a few *Be A Detective* questions typed on card to encourage pupils to find out more about the country and its culture. To develop general geographical skills we displayed a compass with questions to encourage pupils to work out how to use it to identify direction, for example, *Which direction is Kenya from the United Kingdom?* This part of the display became a permanent fixture with questions changing to suit units.

Coherence is the key

Some general points to note about a learning area:

- Store resources for the subject at the learning area and clearly label them so that pupils know where to find textbooks and equipment.

- Wall display, books and other items on the surface display should follow the same theme.
- Include a variety of pupils' work, attractively mounted and clearly labelled.
- Displaying the learning intention and success criteria where relevant gives purpose to the work on display and reinforces pupil involvement in assessment. Also this helps clarify the work for pupils, teachers or visitors viewing the display.
- Carefully selected items on display help provoke pupils' interest and questions.
- Thought-provoking questions on the wall and display surface draw pupils into thinking more deeply about the subject and promote enquiry.
- Interesting and relevant activities help pupils develop various skills whilst working at their own pace. Activities can provide opportunities to make cross-curricular links as well as to consolidate, extend and revise learning.

There is, of course, some work involved in setting up a learning area but little on-going maintenance. Changes in wall display and displayed resources such as books/equipment/ artefacts occur naturally as the class units change. Once independent activities have been devised, they can be ongoing throughout a unit of work and some may only need to be varied slightly for a different unit of work.

Everything you need

In the following 4 chapters I'll tell you how to put together effective learning areas for your classroom. By way of example, I have chosen maths, literacy, science, history, geography and R.E.

I will provide:

- lists of the most useful resources
- ideas for purposeful, interactive displays
- suggestions for activities that encourage pupils to do some hands-on learning. These activities link the interactive display and the resources and make the learning areas come to life. The activities can be adapted for different ages and abilities.

 Throughout the chapters that follow, for quick and easy reference to the many practical ideas for either a display or an activity to include in a learning area, you will see this icon.

 All ideas are intended to be adaptable to suit key stage 1 or key stage 2 unless you see either of the KS1 or KS2 icons.

How you lay out each area is up to you. The lists of ideas are not meant to be exhaustive. They aim is to start you off and inspire you to create the classroom that's right for you.

Don't be overwhelmed

You don't have to do this all at once.

- Decide your priorities – what needs to be done first?
- Everything does not need to be completely in place ready for the first day of term.
- Aim to complete the set-up of one or two curriculum areas really well.
- Build on areas as time goes by.
- Adapt the ideas in this section to suit your teaching style and your pupils.

Chapter 3

PUTTING TOGETHER THE LITERACY LEARNING AREA

Literacy as an area will undoubtedly occupy a large part of your classroom. This is expected and if you develop it to its full advantage, the result will be a physical environment that shouts that you and your pupils are readers and writers.

The following areas should be visible in your classroom:

- class library
- writing area
- listening area.

Literacy resources to use time and again

There will be plenty of resources that you will probably want to stash away in a teacher's cupboard or on shelves, such as teachers' books for schemes and photocopiable workbooks for phonics, spelling and grammar that you will pull out as and when needed. I often forget about the wealth of resources tucked away in my cupboard and only occasionally, when I decide to have a rummage, do I discover or remember great activities that I regret not having used.

One day (during half term), I finally put together a collection of useful resources and I am now the proud owner of activities and games for spelling/phonics, grammar and punctuation; nothing fancy, just worksheets, either homemade or photocopied from various books, plus crosswords, word searches and puzzles from websites. These help children practise the basic skills they will always need to develop no matter what the teaching scheme or curriculum and so have seen me through changes in school, year group, English curriculum and teaching trends. They have also been invaluable when I've covered for a colleague at short notice. To save photocopying them over and over, I laminate and provide a dry-wipe marker to go with the activity. Pupils seem to have much more enthusiasm for the activities this way. They complete, show and then erase, ready for the next person.

I am always on the look out in charity shops for games such as 'Boggle', 'Word Yahtzee' and 'Junior Scrabble' that support literacy skills. (I'm sure that there are more modern similar games – I seem to have an attachment to those from my own childhood.) Depending on how you run your classroom and organise your lessons, if you have these types of activities, organise them into categories and put them somewhere accessible to pupils, perhaps a shelf in your class library (if big enough) or under the whiteboard. Don't hoard gems like this; they are perfect for support or extension activities.

Categorising your class library

I have tried several ways to categorise the class library.

1   Organising books on shelves to look like a traditional library with labels (sometimes alphabetically ordered) defining categories and book stands separating sections, but no defined levelling.
2   Books organised according to level of difficulty by colour coding with stickers, separated into categories and placed on the shelves in labelled plastic baskets.
3   Books on shelves sorted from easiest to most difficult reading levels, left to right.

My favourite is the first, purely because it looks and works most like a public library – the feel that I always aim to create. However, your school may have a policy on levelling books that will dictate which method you use.

Most popular book categories

Key stage 1

Fiction:	Non-fiction:
chapter books	animals
fairy/traditional tales	atlases
favourite authors	dictionaries
favourite characters	encyclopaedias
poetry	nature and weather
picture books	people and places
plays	sport
rhymes and songs	transport
stories from other cultures	

Other:

   class-made books
   free choice (a miscellaneous collection)
   magazines
   reading scheme

Key stage 2

Fiction:	Non-fiction:
fantasy	atlases
historical fiction	autobiographies
modern fiction	biographies
mysteries	dictionaries
myths and legends	encyclopaedias
picture books	history

continued over the page . . .

Fiction:	Non-fiction:
play scripts	geography
poetry	science and nature
science fiction	sport
stories from a range of cultures	
traditional tales	

(At KS2, rather than listing all topics, pupils should be able/learning to categorise under more general headings.)

Other:

      class-made books
      miscellaneous
      magazines

Genres from the 'real world' are great to have samples of in your class library such as newspapers and magazines, brochures, maps and guides, relevant information/articles printed from the internet, cookbooks, menus and catalogues. Pupils will enjoy and get involved in looking for these examples when they're at home or out and about. The downside though is that you can end up with piles of clutter that either gets lost, or sits untidily on shelves and gets ignored. Hang a labelled pocket chart for these additional class library resources or store in labelled magazine files.

Draw pupils' attention with categories such as:

- Books Getting Lots of BUZZ
- Classics – Characters you've got to meet
- Class Picks – Books that have changed our thinking
- For . . . fans (insert popular author/series)
- Journey Books (books that immerse you in a new country or setting).

Create inviting library walls

The walls of the class library should look inviting, enticing your pupils to enter the world of books. If there is a display board above the bookshelves, use it for pupils' writing, book reviews, class-made books or a relevant book-themed display, such as exhibiting an author or artwork related to a book. Save some space for informational and instructional signs/posters that help pupils learn how to use their class library effectively.

 Display posters and questions that give pupils guidance on their choice of reading material.

Create a *Making a good book choice* poster that outlines the steps pupils should take to select an appropriately levelled book. For example,

    Once you have chosen a book, ask yourself these questions to check that it is right for you: Do you understand what the book is about from the title? Have you read and understood the blurb? Look at the first few pages. Can you read most of the words?

Incorporate questions on the wall (mounted to stand out) such as:

How many different types of book have you read?

Which is your favourite genre?

Is there someone who interests you from the past? Look for a biography about them.

Bring to pupils' attention the different book genres. This will help them when browsing categories in the library and as a result, they will be more likely to vary their choice of book.

Make attractive A4 posters containing definitions of book genres and possibly pictures of example book covers, for example autobiography, historical fiction, poetry, traditional folk stories, non-fiction and classic fiction. In addition, for younger children and EAL pupils, be sure to include pictures/images on category labels on the library bookshelves that help explain what they will find in the section.

All too often pupils abandon a book and cannot explain why. Help them to express their reasons for this decision.

Create a poster that asks, *Decided to abandon a book*? List the reasons why this might happen (preferably brainstormed initially with the children). For example: Too difficult; Too easy; It's not what I expected; The blurb is better than the book; I don't like the author's style of writing.

Use book or author posters as a simple way to draw in pupils. Place questions around them so that they are more than just posters stuck on a wall to fill space – they are there to inspire and provoke thought:

How many books do you know written by this author?
Have you read them all?
If you could ask this author one question, what would it be?
From looking at the front cover, what do you think this book is about?
Does this poster make you want to read this book?
Find out what the buzz is about?
Have you read the latest book by . . .? What would you rate it out of 10?

Generate debate about books by creating a favourite author graffiti board.

Decide the author by majority vote. Hang plastic pockets containing the author's books around a board and encourage pupils to pin book reviews, illustrations, etc. to the board. For older pupils, make it pupil-led and as current as possible, perhaps including snippets from the author's website and published book reviews. Pupils could post questions, predictions or opinions about the book for classmates to respond to.

Draw attention to books

The surface display for the class library quite obviously consists of books. Select them thoughtfully, including both fiction and non-fiction, and link them to current study in all curriculum areas. Drawing children's interest can be as simple as standing books attractively on the shelves or changing them frequently. In addition to published books, display books the pupils have written, perhaps a class book of poems or stories on a theme.

 Create a reading buzz in your classroom by displaying class *Book Picks*.

Allow pupils to take turns creating a display of their favourite titles (the way bookshops or DVD rental shops do sometimes), for example, *Gaya's Picks*. Get the class to vote on their favourite titles and display the *Top Ten* or *Best-sellers*. This could be expanded to giving awards to books using categories such as Best Illustrations, Best Series, Most Humorous and Best Historical Fiction.

Class library activities

Don't kill it! There isn't really any need to create activities for the class library – the prompts and questions around the library will be enough. The most important thing is that pupils are simply reading.

Resourcing an enticing writing area

A writing area should be enticing. Being asked to write can be intimidating and a struggle for some pupils. If you create a special, welcoming area where resources are readily available and well organised, pupils are more likely to want to sit and write. A choice of stationery, writing tools and decorative items (for publishing) should do the trick. For example:

- various types and sizes of paper – lined for letter writing, lined with illustration space, themed with a border or picture, greeting cards
- pencils, rulers and erasers
- coloured pencils, crayons, felt-tip pens, gel pens, calligraphy pen and ink, dry-wipe markers
- stickers, scissors, stencils, stamps, glue, glitter
- sheets for planning or brainstorming
- mini whiteboards
- pupils' writing folders/journals/books.

Provide relevant, motivating writing aids, such as:

- checklists for fiction and non-fiction writing
- word banks
- blank mini-books
- magnetic words or letters
- story boxes (containing objects to inspire story-writing or pictures offering choices of characters, objects and settings)

- story props (a bag of items such as toys, puppets or pictures that support the telling of a familiar story)
- picture sequences with lines or bubbles for captions
- a choice of book review frameworks.

You might consider additional storage around your writing area, such as a set of trays or drawers on wheels or shelves so that the actual writing table remains uncluttered.

Put the writing on the wall

The success of the writing area depends on how pupils view it. The main goal is simply for children to want to write and making it not appear a task is the most likely way for that to happen. Children should be encouraged to take risks and write freely, ultimately increasing their confidence and independence and hopefully making for a class of children that enjoy any opportunity to write.

If there is space on the wall around this area, put it to good use by creating writing aids such as a word wall, a punctuation checklist poster, a reminder of what a good story includes or a reminder of the writing process. Displaying mounted pieces of pupils' writing in this area or hanging pupil-made books will motivate others to want to write.

Create a clear writing surface

The surface of the writing area is not about display; there should be a clear area, preferably a table, where pupils are invited to sit and write. Activities and prompts can be placed at this area but too much at one time might overwhelm and confuse pupils. You may prefer that the writing area is free of activities and that the children simply write whatever they choose, for example *Have you got a story in your head that has been bursting to come out? Now's the time to enjoy writing it – off you go.* Your decision will no doubt depend on the age of your pupils and how intrinsically motivated they are. However, prompts, objects and pictures for inspiration can all be useful in encouraging pupils to write and enabling them to do it independently. Quite often, creating an idea for a piece of writing is more difficult than the writing itself.

Teacher tales

Wendy, a Year 2 teacher explains, 'I introduced my writing area because I was finding it difficult to manage the number of children who finished their writing early – there were about nine of them and they would come and stand at my desk, waiting for something else to do. So I created a writing area with a few relevant and varied activities. I rotate children working at it (two at a time). If children visit it to cure their "writers' block", they know that their time at the table is limited and so I think that helps them to focus and be more productive. Whilst the writing table is in use, others can visit to take a story box or another activity back to their desk.'

A selection of writing activities

Inspiring story writing

Writing a story 'off the top of your head' can be a difficult task. Give pupils a helping hand with a Story Box or interesting object. Including a specified prompt can give pupils an extra boost in getting started or enable you to control the focus.

On the table, place a Story Box (decorated shoe box) filled with pictures photocopied from books or cut out from magazines/comics of possible characters, everyday items, problem situations and settings. Alternatively, fill it with a mixture of ordinary and unusual items.

From a story box that contains pictures:

> Pick two characters and write a letter from one to the other.
>
> Write and create a filmstrip using a setting, three characters and a problem. The title of the film is . . .

From a story box that contains objects:

> Pick an item from the box. Imagine that it is magic. Write a story about what happens.
>
> Pick an item from the box. Base your story around this item. Begin with the sentence, 'I was woken early one morning with a loud knocking on the front door.'

On the table, place a pair of sunglasses decorated with interesting attachments, for example stickers, ribbon, tissue paper, tin foil.

> Look through the glasses. Can you see the planet that you have just landed on? Where are you? What do you see? Who are you? What are you going to do?

Wrap up a box as a present and place on the table. As the teacher, ask pupils questions:

> This is a gift that has been given to me. Who do you think gave it to me and why? What is in the box? What do you think I should do with it?

Exploring writing genres

Encourage pupils to explore different genres and styles of writing.

Every few weeks put out a basket/tray with contents that highlight a different genre or style of writing the class has studied. It could include: a non-fiction book, poetry, a newspaper or article of interest, a magazine or a set of instructions. Provide an accompanying writing focus, such as:

> Here is a set of instructions for how to get dressed on a cold day. Can you match each instruction to the correct picture?
>
> This is a photograph from a real newspaper. What is happening?
>
> Use a highlighter pen to mark the words in the poem that rhyme.

Look at the example set of instructions. Write your own instructions on how to play a game you have learnt in P.E.

Write a letter of response to this magazine article expressing your point of view.

Read the poem about feelings. Can you replace the poet's feelings with your own?

Pretend you are a news reporter. Write a script to report what happened in assembly today/during a recent school sporting event.

Objects for inspiration do not have to be restricted to story writing. Place a piece of kitchen equipment on the table such as a sieve, whisk or mixing bowl.

Use this strip of drawings to help you make up a recipe. Write short instructions to go with the pictures.

Writing extension

The writing area could be used for specific extension activities, perhaps for a shared book.

Look at this paragraph from our shared book. Some of the describing words are missing. Can you fill in these gaps with your own describing words so that the paragraph makes sense?

Look at what is going on in this picture from our shared book. Write how the character feels.

Reread paragraph x, chapter x of our class book. Notice how the author uses adjectives and similes to describe the setting. Write a paragraph where you describe a setting, perhaps arriving at a beautiful holiday destination or the scenery from a train window – try to use adjectives and similes in your writing.

One of the themes in this book is . . . Write about a time when something similar happened to you/when you felt . . .

Cross-curricular writing

Look out for ways to make cross-curricular use of the writing area.

Place a photograph or picture on the writing table with a prompt:

This drawing shows a scene from The Great Fire of London. Write a conversation that took place. Who is talking? What are they talking about?

Study the hieroglyphic code. Can you decode it or make up your own code?

Look at the photograph of our local area. Write a poem about what you see.

Look carefully at the book cover of a book you are reading/have recently read. Can you design a different cover for the book?

Draw a picture and leave it in the tray for a classmate to write a story about.

From the tray, take a picture that one of your classmates has drawn and use it to help you write a story.

Teacher tales

'For me, the writing table is all about creativity and free choice', says Maroulla, a Year 6 teacher. 'My children think that it is so special just because they can choose fancy paper and glitter for publishing work. I never see them take so much pride in their writing as when they're sat at that table. I never specify what they should do there. There's one poster above the table that gives suggestions of types of writing they could try, but that's it. It's quite surprising what they sometimes come up with.'

A space for listening

The listening area is really just a grand name for a cassette/CD player with a few pairs of headphones anywhere in the room where there is space. I think it works best in the class library – a comfortable space for children to sit and listen. If you don't have space for the listening area to have a permanent home, put batteries in the player, store it on an open shelf and make the listening area a portable area.

Most useful resources:

- CD player or tape player/recorder
- Headphones
- Multi-user adaptor
- Blank CDs or cassettes
- Pointer
- As many recorded text sets as possible, such as fiction, non-fiction, poems, rhymes and songs (some in languages other than English).

Prompt independent listening

Display permanent signs or prompts to guide children in carrying out a listening activity independently. For example:

Sit back and enjoy this week's book.

Choose a book to listen to. Use the pointer to follow the words as you listen.

As you listen to the story, jot down any vocabulary that you struggled to understand. Look the words up in the dictionary later.

The listening area should not be used solely for literacy activities. There are many ways to incorporate other subjects at the listening area. Place plastic wallets/pouches in a container labelled for different focuses or subjects such as, 'maths: listening area', 'music: listening area'. In each wallet, include a tape or CD and questions or prompts on a card.

- *Maths:*
  Invite pupils to record their own maths problem on to the tape or provide teacher-read maths problems on the tape.
- *Music:*
  Provide a variety of music with prompts for pupils to consider instruments that can be heard, repeated rhythms, speed of music, loud or soft sounds, etc. Pictures/icons of instruments could be included for pupils to match to what they hear. Pupils could be prompted to 'Paint or draw with sound' and express through art what they feel when they listen to the music.
- *Languages:*
  Include tapes of people speaking in other languages that may be familiar or unfamiliar to pupils. If pupils have family members who speak a language other than English, invite them to make a recording in their language. These recordings could serve as an aid for EAL pupils and as a way to increase pupils' awareness of languages that exist within their classroom community. Accompany with questions about how the language sounds. Is it similar or different from their own language? Also provide a transcript to look at once they have completed the activity that translates the recording.
- *Relaxation station:*
  Provide CDs of various calming music for 'time out' or 'chill out time'.
- *Science:*
  Provide a tape of sound effects. Pupils could draw pictures of what they identify the sounds to be, describe in writing or describe the sound to a friend who then has to try to guess the sound effect without hearing it.
- *Humanities:*
  Include stories from other cultures and various periods in time. Create quizzes to go with recent lessons.

Encourage independent role-play

At key stage 1, an allocated area for role-play might be a standard part of your classroom. It is usually hard to make space for this in a key stage 2 classroom, nor is it necessarily expected. This does not mean though that pupils would not benefit from or enjoy it; so don't rule it out. Rather than a permanent space allocated for role-play, you could integrate resources into an already existing learning area to encourage role-play linked to a class topic. For example, if studying another country, set up props in the maths area and invite children to play 'Bureau de Change'. Another option is to provide a box containing a selection of general props for role-play and dramatisation, for example puppets, hats and old clothes. To really stretch children's imaginations, provide old household objects such as a mop and bucket, an old telephone with pencils and a memo pad or an old paper fan and umbrella.

Some suggestions for role-play themes:

- post office
- travel agent's
- airport check-in
- doctor's/dentist's surgery/optician's shop
- vets
- museum
- toy shop
- café
- supermarket
- garden centre
- recycling centre
- fire engine/bus
- rainforest

Chapter 4

CONSTRUCTING THE MATHS LEARNING AREA

How many maths resources do you *really* need?

Maths seems to be the subject accompanied by the most resources, and it's easy to end up with multiple baskets and trays full of the same sorts of items, such as various types of counting aids. Work out how much you realistically need for your class and then offer the rest to someone else, rather than allowing them to gather dust at the back of the shelf. Much will depend on the amount of room you have. Generally, it's best to only keep resources in your classroom that the children regularly use. If other larger pieces of equipment and resources for future units can be stored in a central area, just bring them to your room as and when you need them.

Top 10 classroom resources

Key stage 1	Key stage 2
1 bead strings	1 digit cards/number fans
2 number lines	2 large 1–100 number square
3 number fans	3 base ten blocks
4 place value materials	4 mini whiteboards
5 interlocking cubes	5 place value cards
6 number cards 1–100	6 fractions tiles
7 large dice	7 plastic money
8 2D and 3D shapes	8 die
9 mini whiteboards	9 various sized squared/dot paper
10 plastic money	10 Number line (including negatives, fractions, decimals, %)

Keep teaching aids to hand

Resources that you need for mental maths or demonstration should be kept to hand so they don't get mixed up with general resources or lost. Store near your main teaching area or the interactive whiteboard; keep smaller items in hanging pockets or in a basket.

Most useful items

- counting stick
- OHP equipment such as OHT counters, calculator, protractor, set square, etc.

- stop watch
- 'follow me'/loop cards
- true/false cards
- large teaching clock
- playing cards
- hundreds pocket chart with reversible numbers
- maths washing line
- flash cards
- whiteboard dice

Maths wall display can be more than 3D shapes

Children's maths work does not always obviously lend itself to display. Everyday work, such as pupils' written responses to word problems or 'sums' are hard to make visually attractive. It's easier to make displays out of work related to units such as handling data, shape and space, symmetry, fractions and maths investigations. However, it is refreshing to display maths in a way that focuses on the process rather than the finished product. This makes for a more interactive display, challenging pupils to think of alternative methods.

 Create a display from even the least likely unit of work.

Display a maths problem that pupils were given, large enough to be read from a distance, along with the varying methods they used to solve it. Include explanations and prompts such as:

Look at the different ways we solved the problem.

How would you solve the problem?

Would you use one of these methods, or another way?

Have a go at solving this problem.

 Add variation with a display that hangs from the ceiling or from a washing line.

 Make concertina books of children's number sentences and hang them from string. Use a strip of card folded into three sections with dots or pictures that children have coloured to represent a number sentence such as '3, 2, and 5'. Underneath, the child or teacher could expand to '3 + 2 = 5'.

 Ask children to write story problems in the form of a mini-book with pictures.

 To save time in the long run, create large interactive displays as permanent fixtures that are altered slightly every now and then.

This one is called *Calculation Station*. Make a giant calculator out of card. Include a screen, a keypad showing the digits zero to nine and the functions divide, multiply, subtract, add and equals. Make a few extra sets of digits and an extra set of functions that can be pinned onto the 'screen' to pose a calculation. The calculator screen can pose a different calculation for children to work out each day/week and can easily vary in level of difficulty by being a single or multi-step calculation. Display a selection of possible answers on cards to the right of the calculator. Children work out which they think is the correct answer, write their name and suggestion on a slip of paper and place in a container/bag. Calculations could be teacher-created or children could take it in turns to make one up for the rest of the class to solve.

Teacher tales

'I don't enjoy changing all of my display boards every six weeks or so', says Lori, a teacher of nine years. 'This year, I made the board behind my maths area an interactive display by creating "Maths Flower Power". I made a large colourful flower. A digit from 0 to 9 was printed on each petal with "10" in the flower centre. Around the flower were questions such as, "How many different ways can you make 10?" "4 +? = 10", "What do you notice about 1 + 9 and 9 + 1? Can you make similar patterns?" I found that as a Year 2 teacher, I would spend the first term of every school year attempting to drill number bonds to 10. This display was the most encouraging way I found of doing it. Also, not only did it look bold and enticing, it could stay there! Once the class had mastered number bonds to 10, I varied it to number bonds to 20. A Year 4 colleague of mine created a similar display for multiplication tables depicting a favourite character. Its arms, legs, fingers, toes, etc., showed the digits 0 to 12 and the body centre the number to multiply by.'

Use posters as a teaching aid to demonstrate difficult concepts.

Posters can be useful, although you should be wary of overdoing them – too many and children won't take notice of them. Rotating posters and drawing pupils' attention to the change will give them more impact. Posters can be useful for helping pupils understand concepts they find a struggle.

Some of the most useful posters demonstrate:

- digit and word correspondence on a number line.
- place value
- months of the year on a calendar or birthday 'train'
- addition and subtraction fact families.
- simple fractions.

Some of the most useful posters demonstrate:

- negatives and decimals, fraction and percentage equivalents on a number line
- measurement conversions
- capacity equivalents.

Posters demonstrating vocabulary related to each mathematical operation are useful to both key stages, as well as times tables posters, telling time posters, a large 1–100 number square and shape recognition posters.

Add something special to your maths area with an engaging teacher-made poster.

 Create a large, 5x5 grid with 5 rows and 5 columns. Label the columns (from left to right) 1, 2, 3, 4 and 5. Label the rows (from top to bottom) A, B, C, D and E. On the grid, place removable pictures. These could be thematic or pictures of random items. Surround the grid with questions such as:

> The train is at A4, true or false?
>
> Where is the boat?
>
> Is the bicycle at D2?

 Using a rectangular, A2 piece of card, create a 5x5 grid with 5 rows and 5 columns. Label the columns (from left to right) C1, C2, C3, C4 and C5. Label the rows (from top to bottom) R1, R2, R3, R4 and R5. Fill the boxes of the grid with playing cards (do not include the Jacks, Queens or Kings from the pack). Surround the grid with questions to challenge children and develop their skills at reading coordinates, for example:

> What is 'R2, C4' multiplied by 'R4, C1'?
>
> Can you give the coordinates of an even number?
>
> Is 'R3, C2' a multiple of 2?

Use questioning to make sure that items on display remain fresh and challenging.

A washing line with hanging number cards is useful as an interactive display item. It can be in constant use by changing the order of the numbers and the numbers themselves to show sequences, negative numbers, etc., and putting questions or a *'Washing Line Challenge of the Week'* alongside such as:

> Can you order these jumbled up cards 0 to 10?
>
> Find the odd/even numbers in this pile and hang them in sequence on the line.
>
> On a piece of paper, write which number comes 2 before the first number on the line. Place your suggestion in the box.

Provide constant challenges for pupils by displaying a Hundred Square 1–100 Pocket Chart and accompanying it with questions. (Pockets contain numbered cards that are coloured differently on the reverse side to highlight number patterns.) Include questions such as:

> Can you find multiples of 5? Flip the cards to show. The first two have been done for you. Do you notice a pattern?
>
> Look at today's/this week's pattern on the chart. Can you describe the rule? Jot your suggestion down on paper and place in the 'I solved it' box.

If you don't have a 1–100 pocket chart like the one described, but you have a 1–100 number square poster, provide a basket of coloured 1–100 digit cards and sticky tack. Pupils use them to cover the numbers on the square as a way of highlighting a pattern.

Use the surrounding surface effectively

There are three main elements that make a good maths surface display area:

- non-fiction books with maths themes
- maths storybooks/number rhyme books
- thoughtfully selected resources accompanied by questions, tasks and/or information.

Look for non-fiction books with maths themes

These are not always in abundance, but can be found. Most common are books on shape and space, measures and money. If you cannot find books that are solely maths-themed, look for non-fiction books picturing everyday things that could be viewed in a mathematical sense, for example buildings/architectural structures for angles, road signs for symmetry and shape. Exploring maths through independent reading is an alternative, appealing way for a child to absorb new concepts and/or revise what they already know. It encourages children to read non-fiction if they are reluctant to do so independently.

Alongside non-fiction maths books, display prompts or challenges on a card.

> How about reading a maths book for a change?
>
> Using pictures, show/find and write about three facts that you didn't already know.
>
> Write a maths question for a friend. They must be able to find the answer in this book.

Include maths storybooks/number rhyme books

These are engaging and can be used to explore maths concepts at any level. Even if the book is read purely for enjoyment, the child still absorbs vocabulary and visual clues. Maths storybooks usually introduce a problem. This encourages pupils to think about why and how it needs solving. They can investigate different strategies to find a solution.

Put a storybook on display that wouldn't necessarily be considered maths-themed; it could be a familiar class favourite. Challenge the pupils to find an element of maths within it.

Include a prompt such as:

> Is there maths in this book? Can you use it to make up a mathematical question or a problem for a friend?

Display a *Maths Storybook of the Week* (or every few weeks).

Share the storybook with the class, identifying the maths problem that it presents. Have pupils explore the book with a partner (mixed ability pairs tend to work best for this). At an appropriate time of the week, hold a class discussion for pairs to reveal solutions found. Pupils could present their findings in various ways, for example, through illustrations, role-play or demonstration using practical resources/equipment.

Hands-on maths learning

By setting out resources that you want to draw pupils' attention to on a surface top and accompanying them with tasks or questions on a small whiteboard/pin board or card, you can involve pupils in hands-on learning. The resources could be linked to a current unit of work or could be based around something the class needs to practise further.

 Help pupils to link a maths concept like fractions with something in real life or a real life problem to be solved.

Display items in a transparent container, for example, 12 cubes, 50 sweets, 100 small stones or a segmented bar of chocolate (guaranteed to get pupils' interest). Include a prompt card, for example:

Count the cubes. How many is one quarter/three fifths/a half?

What fraction of the sweets are red?

Share the cubes/sweets with a friend. Do you both have the same amount? Why/why not?

If you share the bar of chocolate with one other person and you have two thirds of it, who has the most? How many pieces do you have?

 Encourage pupils to carry out practical work focusing on units that tend to get less class time devoted to them.

Display a variety of measuring equipment, for example a tape measure, a ruler, a metre stick and a piece of string.

Look at the list of objects/pictures. Which unit of measurement would you choose for measuring each one? (Measurement choices could be provided, for example, mm, cm, m, and km.)

Find 10 things to measure in the room. You must use each piece of measuring equipment.

 Encourage pupils to take a hands-on approach to capacity. It doesn't have to be a current unit for pupils to explore and practise basic skills in this area of maths.

Display containers of various shapes and sizes.

Which holds more/less? How can you find out?

Pour the water from one container to another. What do you notice?

Can you measure out . . . ml of water?

Use the surface display area as a mini shop to develop money-handling skills in a fun, practical way.

Make a shop sign and display items with prices attached. Perhaps use plastic fruit and vegetables or everyday school resources, such as a packet of colouring pencils, an eraser, pencil sharpener, etc.

> You have 5 pounds to spend. What will you buy? Will you have any change? If so, how much?

Set out shopping lists; give pupils a specified amount to spend.

> Find the total cost of the items on the list. Have you got enough money to buy everything? Will you have change and how much? What will you choose to buy if you don't have enough money?

Chapter 5

BUILDING THE SCIENCE LEARNING AREA

Keep the best science resources to hand

Science resources are usually stored in a central area unless there are some that are specific to your year group units. But even then, if you don't have to, don't hold class sets of resources in your classroom unless your pupils are actually using them. If possible, keep just a few general science resources in your room, enabling pupils to creatively carry out a variety of learning area activities. Pupils are more likely to want to 'do' science if there is further opportunity for science investigation and if resources are not restricted to whole class lessons.

Most useful general science resources

Key stage 1 and 2

- magnifying glasses
- observation/Petri dishes
- thermometers
- pipettes/syringes
- a microscope
- scales
- force meters
- tape measures
- graduated measuring jugs/cylinders
- variety of containers (some waterproof)

Organising resources

If you don't have a lot of room for storing science resources or if your school isn't very well resourced, you could put together a 'science box' containing unit-related items that can be collected (by you and the children) for little or no cost. The idea is that pupils independently select items of their choice when carrying out learning area activities. You do not need many of each item because the whole class will not be using the box at the same time.

What to include in a science box

- elastic bands
- corks
- string

- small mats of different surfaces
- collection of materials/objects to illustrate particular properties
- metals and non-metals
- mirrors
- a torch
- objects that float/sink
- sponges
- sieves with differently-sized holes
- small containers or bags of sand, soil, sugar, small stones
- possible conductors/non-conductors of electricity – piece of wood, aluminium foil, plastic spoon, wire, key, paper, scissors, nail, paper clip, polystyrene
- magnets
- batteries
- bulbs
- different lengths of plastic-coated wire
- different coloured Perspex sheets
- toys that move in different ways
- balls
- plasticine
- cotton wool
- polythene bags

Scientific enquiry questions

The science learning area should provide a range of purely enquiry-based questions that pupils can explore independently or in pairs/small groups. They should not require teacher set-up and most of the equipment should be available in the science box or around the classroom.

Example questions

- Which of two bags is the strongest?
- Can seeds grow anywhere?
- How can you keep a hot drink warm for longer?
- Which materials are attracted to a magnet?
- Which ball is the bounciest?
- Which of the cars will travel furthest?
- Are everyone's hands the same size?
- Which material is best for mopping up water?
- Does coffee dissolve in cold water?
- What happens when you hit a small drum compared with a big drum?

Organisational tips

Scientific enquiry questions could direct pupils to particular boxes of resources to use to investigate the question. All the questions could be displayed as a set in a box or you could place a different card out each week. I prefer to have all of the cards out because it's fun for groups of children to work on different things at one time; less of the same resources are needed and it helps children to apply a range of skills, some of which may have been learnt from another unit. Either provide a sheet for a specific way of recording/investigating or encourage pupils to make up their own method. To save on preparation time, pupils could follow the same procedure for every investigation. Write the titles on a piece of display card and permanently place at the area. For example, *What I will use*, *What I predict*, *What I did*, *What I observed*, *Why I think this happened*.

Teacher tales

'I used to feel guilty that I wasn't carrying out enough science investigations with my Year 4 class', says Catherine, a teacher of 4 years. 'The truth is that I would fully intend for the children to carry out an investigation as part of their science lesson and then something would inevitably happen that day that would prevent me from getting organised in time – usually an unexpected lunchtime meeting or having to deal with a child during break time when I had planned to set up. When I was introduced to the idea of a science box, science in my classroom was transformed! Instead of the "doing" part of science being a controlled, whole-class, once in a while experience, it became the norm and wasn't restricted to science lessons either. We would have "investigation time", when a group of children would use the science box to carry out their own investigations, either something they devised themselves linked to our current unit or initiated by an "investigation card". I do still organise whole-class investigations, but at least if I don't get around to it, my class aren't missing out on hands-on science.'

Interactive, informative science displays

Science display lends itself to being both informative and interactive. It's a great way to reinforce concepts and encourage pupils to ask questions, revise and reflect on what they have learnt.

Add a 'match up' element to an informative display. This will encourage pupils to really engage with what they are seeing displayed on the wall.

Display large pictures of the components of an animal food chain/the life cycle of a flowering plant/an electrical circuit/mini-beasts, etc. Make removable parts or labels and challenge pupils to put things in the correct order or to match things up.

Can you match each part of the flowering plant with its job description?

Can you put the pictures of these solids, liquids and gases inside the correct circles?

Study the animal pictures and the animal skeletons. Which skeleton belongs with which animal?

Can you put the planets in the correct order from the Sun?

Match each mini-beast to its home.

Match the type of sense to the correct body part picture.

Decide which group – shiny, rough or dull each type of paper should be sorted into.

Place the picture of the food in the child's tummy if you think it is important for a balanced diet.

Place one of these tick symbols on the picture of the object if you think it uses electricity and a cross if you think it doesn't.

What to do if display boards are out of pupils' reach

Obviously, the match-up idea is only effective if pupils can physically manipulate the labels on the board. If this isn't possible, the same display could be created, but instead of physically manipulating the pieces, pupils jot their answers on to an index card and post them into a post-box attached to the bottom of the board. Another option is to create a simplified version of the display on a large piece of card/poster-board that can be attached to the wall at pupils' level or mounted stiffly and propped up on the display surface. If removable pieces are laminated, this is something that you can bring out year after year.

When recounting an investigation, use photographs, quotes and pupils' opinions to liven up the display.

Include photographs of the children working at different stages of an investigation with speech bubbles to show thoughts and explain what happened. For example:

Rachel and Amish observe closely as Faisal takes the temperature of the water.

Look how the coffee has stayed lumpy in the cold water.

(photograph of pupil with speech bubble) 'I predict that the sugar will dissolve when it's added to the water.'

Teacher tales

'Using photographs in a display is nowhere near as much work as it sounds', says Year 1 teacher, Rhianne. 'As long as you remember to take plenty of photos while the children are carrying out an investigation and also note down a few of their comments and responses to questions, it's easy. I print all of the photographs on the school printer and lay them out in some sort of chronological order on a table. After looking at them for just a few minutes, the speech bubbles seem obvious. I actually enjoy writing them, as I know the children get so much pleasure from seeing pictures of themselves on the wall and reading what I've written in their speech bubble. I'm pretty certain that my class would not show an interest in reading a recount of an investigation if it wasn't presented in this way, but hey, whatever works.'

Include pupil voice as a way of really making science enquiry-based.

Create columns on your science display board and add headings such as, *What do we want to find out? What do we predict/think will happen? What did we observe/notice?* Pupils place sticky notes containing their own ideas and observations in the appropriate columns.

Draw pupils' attention by pinning things of interest to the display board for observation.

For example, if studying micro-organisms, place food to be observed in clear, plastic sandwich bags.

> Observe the bread over the next few days. Keep a log in your science journal in any way you like to record what happens.

Teacher tales

'I came up with the idea of pinning items to my science display board because my classroom was tiny and I didn't have space for a display surface in front of it, says Pam, a Year 3 teacher. "I'm the science coordinator at my school so I had to try to set an example for colleagues, showing them that science display could include points of interest in even a tiny classroom. When we studied plants, I put seeds in 'Ziploc' bags and pinned them to the display board. It actually worked really well because the bags kept them moist. To create varying conditions, I covered one with black paper and left one of the bags open, so there wouldn't be any moisture. The children were so intrigued by the bags. I once overheard a child telling a child in another class, 'In our class, we have real science on the walls!'"'

Find ways to attract young scientists

A good science surface display area contains:

- non-fiction science books
- thoughtfully selected resources accompanied by questions, tasks and information.

Non-fiction science books

You can probably find plenty of science reference books that coordinate with the units you cover and encourage pupils to find out more about a topic. However, quite often the books available to you look old-fashioned and unappealing, so pupils are unlikely to choose to remove them from the class library shelves. Even if the book doesn't look exciting, just selecting it for the display surface and accompanying it with a simple *Come and look* sign or *Did you know . . .?* is invitation enough for pupils to take an interest. Look out for story-themed, non-fiction science books that are now widely available. These are appealing to even the most reluctant 'scientist'.

Alongside non-fiction science books, display prompts or questions on a card.

> Complete the scientist challenge by finding the answer to this question . . .
>
> Find out a surprising fact and share it with a friend.
>
> Choose one of these books to read.
>
> Write a 'Did you know?' question and display it next to the book.

Resources for display

Science is made so much more interesting when there is something set out that invites pupils to explore. Research shows that the most important science skill to develop at primary level is that of enquiry and giving pupils the independence to do this is incredibly motivating. There are ways to display items that will be relevant to any unit of work and certain to promote enquiry-based learning.

An observation tray and a magnifying glass encourages pupils to take more than a passing glance at items on display. Change the items on the tray depending on your current unit.

Things to observe:

- a plant/germinating seed
- worms or woodlice in a re-created natural habitat
- fake animal models/skeletons
- a piece of bread/cheese
- a melting ice cube
- a beaker containing a solid of some sort mixed with water, for example, sand or flour
- a tooth or penny in Coca-Cola

Accompany the observation tray with signs such as:

> Come and take a closer look
>
> What's going on in our lab today?
>
> What science is taking place today?
>
> Be a scientist – observe

Store pupils' observation logs/science journals in a container nearby for them to access easily when they visit the area. This will help pupils to develop the habit of using the logs without it seeming like a chore or involving lots of organisation on your part. To encourage pupils to use their science journals, include signs such as:

> Quick! Record the science before things change.
>
> Draw a diagram or make notes about what you see/observe.
>
> See something interesting? Don't forget to log it.

Encourage pupils to investigate using all of their senses.

Create a 'Feely Bag' to draw attention to selected objects and probe pupils to ask questions. If a bag isn't always appropriate for the type of object you want to 'showcase', try a box with material over the top and a slit cut for pupils' hands to fit through. Include questions on a card that can apply to anything you put in the bag:

> Is it soft or hard? Is it cold or warm? Is it rough or smooth? Is it dry or wet? Can you draw what you think is inside? Describe what you can feel to a friend.

Create a 'Smell It If You Dare' tray/challenge. Children try to identify a liquid/food/material by its smell. Place in Petri dishes or bottles and either cover or include an eye mask for children to wear to carry out the task. Something similar could be set up for taste testing, but don't forget to consult parents beforehand and check for allergies.

Place a mixture of items that can be used to make noise on a covered tray/in a bag. Pupils work in pairs to 'Name That Noise' with one child using the items to make noises and the other child listening in order to guess what is making the noise. For example, use sandpaper, bubble wrap, elastic band around card, a lid snapping shut, a small balloon, foil, etc.

Create a 'Memory Mystery' tray with a certain number of items (which could be unit linked) on a tray. This could be used as a partner game with children taking it in turns to remove an item and the other guessing what it is. Alternatively, leave the tray of items on display and remove something each day. Pupils write what they think is missing and post in a post box.

Much of science is about classifying the world around you into categories. Help pupils develop their understanding of this by sorting objects or pictures into groups.

Provide pictures for pupils to sort into trays/Venn diagram hoops/piles on top of sheets of different coloured paper. Alternatively, enable pupils to search through magazines or computer clip-art to find their own items to sort. Perhaps incorporate a challenge such as, *Work with a friend. Who can sort the items the fastest?*

Task examples:

> Can you sort the pictures into things that are alive and things that have never been alive?
>
> Some of these things give off light and some of them don't. Can you sort them?
>
> Place the pictures of the food into the correct food group.
>
> Look at what is happening in the picture, then sort into reversible change and irreversible change.
>
> From this pile of items, find things that you think will float and things that you think will sink.
>
> Look at the pictures of living things. Can you work out a way of grouping them? For example, has wings, has eight legs, etc.

Can you sort the objects according to their properties, for example, rough, shiny, hard, magnetic, etc.?

Perhaps incorporate a challenge such as: work with a friend. Who can sort the items the fastest?

Exemplify science that pupils have been learning about and invite pupils to visit the learning area to *Have a go*.

Can you shine the torch on the model earth to show the sun's position at different times of the day?

Play the instrument. Can you hear and feel the vibrations?

Can you make the bulb light to make this a complete circuit?

Use the torch and the paper to create a shadow.

Investigate these toys. Do you think any of them have parts that move? How might you make them move?

Use the magnet to pick up items from the tray. Which are metals/non-metals?

Use the sieves to separate the rocks, pebbles and gravel.

Can you use the paper fasteners to put the paper skeleton together correctly?

Chapter 6

PIECING TOGETHER LEARNING AREAS FOR HISTORY, GEOGRAPHY AND R.E.

Depending on how your school organises the curriculum, you may not be required to teach geography, history and R.E. all in the same term or half term. But there is no reason why the display in your room can't reflect all three, all year round. There are common elements throughout the three subjects that you can pick out through display. Many of the history, geography and R.E. units we teach are based around significant people, places or events either present day or past, a religion or a culture. Developing common skills such as a sense of chronology, finding evidence and making comparisons is what pulls these three humanities subjects together.

Varied humanities resources

Resources for humanities subjects vary greatly from school to school. For subjects such as maths, English and science, resources seem to be quite clear cut, but for humanities subjects, many of the desired resources are not items that can be ordered from school catalogues, they have to be sought out by teachers. This takes time that we don't always have and we sometimes don't know where to go to find the things we would like.

Resources wish list

History	Geography	R.E.
Historical fiction	Atlases	Religious stories/texts
Artefacts from the past/ present	Artefacts from another country/ society	Religious artefacts
Models (for example transportation)	Models of buildings/of a development	Models of places of worship
Historical maps	Large world/British Isles map	
	Pictorial maps Historical maps Globe Travel brochures/magazines	

continued over the page . . .

History	Geography	R.E.
Music from various periods in time	Music from other countries	Music from other cultures/ various religions
Unit-related textbooks		
Non-fiction books		
Unit-related posters, pictures and photographs		
Videos/DVDs		
ICT software		
Copies of significant documents/letters/diaries, first-hand accounts, newspaper/magazine articles, interview recordings		

Connect learning with wall display

It's not difficult to find ideas for stunning displays on unit themes and I do not intend to compete with all of the fabulous books and websites that do this so well. My aim is to help you integrate and develop the common elements mentioned earlier, so your walls show not just what pupils have been studying, but their depth of thinking around the unit and the links they are able to make between current and previous study or study in other areas.

Teacher tales

'When it comes to history display,' says Year 1 teacher, David, 'there's always something on my classroom wall. I just find that there's so much display opportunity for the units we cover. I seem to create a geography display less often, although I'm not sure why as there are plenty of ideas out there, and if I'm being honest, my efforts for R.E. are a bit rubbish. When we study a religion it's easier, but in general I feel that my classroom walls lack representation of R.E. There is nothing of substance that really shows my pupils are making thoughtful connections between their own lives and lives of others or communicating their opinions. That's what I would aim for.'

Find and consider information through enquiry

Find out what pupils want to know about a unit they are studying. Display the process and then later, the findings.

There's always a phase when a display board is 'under construction' and your pupils have to carry out the work before it can be displayed. Use this time to show pupils' thinking by highlighting the stages in the enquiry process. Split the display board into some or all of the following columns:

What do we know?

What do we want to know?

How will we find out?

How will we present our findings?

As part of the brainstorm process for a unit, each child makes notes of their knowledge, wonderings and ideas on sticky notes and places them in the appropriate column. A range of themes stemming from the unit will naturally emerge from pupils' curiosity about things such as: important events in a period of history, way of life for children in a particular country or during a period of history, key people, religion, language, weather/climate, transport, homes, food and many more. Pupils then turn his/her wondering into a question to be investigated. This enables research to be open-ended and places no limit on how much pupils have to know or on depth of understanding and so is suitable for all ages and abilities.

An alternative approach for pupils to arrive at questions for enquiry is to record, perhaps on large pieces of sugar paper or as a print out, a list of questions that have resulted from a class brainstorm, along with pupil quotes that emerge from discussion. These can be displayed as is, to highlight the beginnings of the enquiry process for a unit.

Another way to show that research is underway is to create a mural that develops as the pupils continually add findings to it. For example, if studying India, the mural background could show a typical landscape and pupils add annotated drawings/paintings/photographs or collage to show aspects mentioned above such as the types of transportation or types of homes.

If appropriate, allow your pupils responsibility for how their findings will be presented either as a class display or as individual/group work. This could be a 'spider web' with the enquiry question in the middle, for example, *What was life like in Victorian times?* and the board split into labelled sections such as: *Type of work*, *Inventions* and *Clothing*. Alternatively, the unit title could be placed in the middle, for example, *Victorian Times* with section headings phrased as questions such as: *Did children go to school?* and *What types of homes did people live in?* The children's findings are then displayed within these sections. If there is too much information to fit this way, display one group's work at a time or challenge children to record findings in various ways, for example, in a booklet that could hang from the display board or ceiling.

Some advice about enquiry-based learning

Asking pupils to come up with their own question about a topic can seem like a good idea, but most often, children's questions stem from concepts, *What is it like?* or *How does it work?* For example, *Which countries were involved in the Second World War? What is the landscape like in this country?* or *How do Muslims worship?* These are valid questions, but we should also encourage questions that explore *why* something is like it is, how something is connected to other things, points of view and change. Pupils should also know that enquiry questions should not be able to be answered with either a simple 'yes' or 'no' or by finding out a fact. For example, instead of 'What is the biggest volcano that has ever erupted?' consider 'Why do some volcanoes erupt and others don't?'

Helping pupils develop an approach to enquiry from a range of perspectives will promote real understanding. I was familiarised with the following set of questions when teaching the International Baccalaureate curriculum. This is something that I now take with me to any unit of work from any curriculum.

- What is it like?
- How does it work?
- Why is it like it is?
- How is it changing?
- How is it connected to other things?
- What are the points of view?
- What is our responsibility?
- How do we know?

(Taken from 'Making the PYP Happen', 2000 International Baccalaureate Organisation, Switzerland)

Depending on how in depth pupils' questions are, they could serve as mini on-going projects to be presented in a way of pupils' choice.

The following are some examples of questions for enquiry. They could be:

- used to help pupils devise their own questions
- adapted to suit a specific unit or year group
- provided as a set of investigation questions at the history/geography/R.E. learning area.

History

What were homes like during Victorian times?

How did early cars work?

Why did the Aztecs make human and animal sacrifices?

How have children's toys changed over time?

How did the explorations of Sir Walter Raleigh contribute to what we know today?

What were some of the points of view about Henry VIII as King?

How could you leave evidence for future generations of what life is like in the 2000s?

How do we know what our town was like during the Second World War?

Geography

What is the weather/climate like in this place?

How have people modified this place to meet their needs?

What natural events cause people to relocate?

Do people who live in the same natural environment always have the same culture?

Is the place I live in similar to or different from this place? How?

How might I spend a day living in this place? What would be the best thing about that day? What would be my greatest problem?

How is the way we live now causing environmental damage?

How do we know how far away this place is?

R.E.

What roles do individuals play in this religion/society?

How do Jewish people celebrate Chanukah?

Why do some Muslim women wear a headdress?

Are there any key people that have shaped this religion?

How are the beliefs, values and norms of a people today connected with their ancestors?

Can I talk about what one of my classmates believes, even though I don't believe in it myself?

How can I be a responsible member of my family/school/faith/world?

How do we know about this religion/culture?

Develop a sense of chronology: timeline

A timeline in your classroom is essential. Everything you study as part of history, geography and R.E. can be related to it, which helps children make the connections that deepen understanding. For example, if a Year 5 class has been studying the Second World War and then moves on to study a country in geography, the timeline acts as a prompt for them to consider what was happening in that country during the Second World War. Was the landscape affected? What was the impact on way of life for people of that country? If a

Year 2 class is studying Christianity, they should use the timeline to highlight how long the religion has existed.

Physically fitting a timeline around your classroom wall can be a challenge. There are ways to combat this problem.

- A concertina timeline takes up less room and looks interesting. This is a folded rectangular strip or several strips joined together with every other section jutting out from the wall (in a 'v' shape).
- *Footprints through time* could meander across the floor, going up the wall. Simply use a large footprint as a template and write on it or stick information to it and laminate.
- A washing (time)line with cards hanging from pegs does not require wall space. It's also flexible, as cards can be added easily. It can be made interactive by inviting children to put recently learnt events in the correct order or to add a fact to a period of time.
- Create a timeline in the corridor outside your room.

Teacher tales

'When devising a timeline I always struggled with the distance between the sections and how much detail to include,' says Year 5 teacher, Selvi. 'If I left enough space between sections to be able to include the detail I wanted, the timeline was far too long for my wall. I decided what worked best was to represent periods as chunks of time, for example Victorians, Tudors, Vikings, but make the scale fairly small and then "magnify" the areas being studied, placing a symbol of a magnifying glass on the timeline and showing that section in detail below.'

What to put on your timeline

Your timeline should include significant periods in time even if they haven't been studied that year as it will help pupils remember what they learnt in previous year groups or familiarise them with things they will later learn.

Begin from the very beginning and label sections as 'number of years ago'. For example, *13 billion years ago: The Big Bang*; *65 million years ago: Dinosaurs became extinct*. A timeline presented in this way helps pupils get an overall sense of chronology.

Be sure to include key events that the class has come across in all three subjects throughout the year. For example, *1929: Britain declared war*; *1963: Martin Luther King made his 'I have a Dream' speech*; *2004: A tsunami devastated Thailand*.

Allow pupils to create personal timelines and family trees by sequencing events in their home or school life and depicting the background of their families. There are endless ways that these can be presented, for example as writing, pictures or photographs, as books, films, posters or concertina timelines that hang from the ceiling.

Make comparisons

Approach the display for any unit in a way that enables comparisons to be made.

Split a display board into *here* and *there* or similarly *then* and *now*. This is another opportunity for pupils to lead their own enquiry. What do they want to know about what is the same and what is different between their own community/country/religion/culture and another (existing or past)? Compare aspects of a period in history to life as they know it today.

Use a world map

Make a large, world map a permanent fixture and a resource in use at all times.

Title your world map with *Where in the world . . .?* changing the end of the question:

- do we come from? (family background/connections)
- is the religion of . . . practised?
- do we speak . . . (language)?
- do we find . . . (a food/animal)?
- is it hot/snowy/has seasons?
- is the country/town . . . located?

In the same way as the timeline, link a magnifying glass symbol to pictures, photographs or information around the edges.

Bring the past to life

Bring the past to life in your classroom with a life size character that 'speaks' to the class.

Ask the children to collage or paint a large character/key person, for example a Tudor figure/ancient Greek, Greek God, Victorian. Add a speech bubble and change it each week with a new fact about the period.

Intrigue pupils with a poster

When first displaying a poster for a unit, cover most of it. Reveal a different section each day and include questions for pupils to consider, either next to the poster or on the whiteboard:

Where do you think this picture was taken?

Go to the world map; put a pin where in the world this is found.

What do you think the people are doing in the picture?

What do you think they believe?

What are they saying to each other?

What are they about to do?

What has happened?

Create a graffiti wall

Reflect the various faiths, cultures, nationalities and languages that exist within the class by allowing pupils to 'graffiti' a wall.

Invite children to bring in photos of their places of worship/their locality/family. Also, use the board and possibly a display table to acknowledge celebrations that take place at different times of the year for different pupils. Items could be brought in such as clothes, food and music. The display area doesn't have to be permanent, perhaps once a month or just at the time of a celebration.

Intrigue pupils with artefacts and pictures

I find the surface displays for history, geography and R.E. to be the most engaging of all the subjects. There are so many elements that can be explored through artefacts and pictures and children are always intrigued by items that are unfamiliar.

Provoke interest by introducing new artefacts in an enticing way.

Pull an item out of a bag each day or every few days and discuss. Alternatively, play a game by placing a few artefacts on a tray, covered with a piece of material. Reveal and allow pupils just a few minutes to look at them. Then question them about what they think they saw.

Invite children to *Be an artefact detective*. This involves them finding out and considering evidence without it seeming like a chore.

Provide a sheet that can be photocopied and placed in a tray that asks questions of an object or picture such as:

> What do you think the artefact is?
>
> Where has it come from?
>
> What do you think it would be used for?'
>
> What material is it made from? Is it new or old?
>
> Which period in time do you think this artefact was made/used? How can you tell?
>
> What does this picture show or tell us about the past?

Similarly, provide pupils with a *What's on display today?* journal, which invites them to explore all sources of information on the table, such as artefacts, photographs and books. How pupils use the journal will obviously vary depending on year group and ability. For example:

> Sketch an artefact on display.
>
> Write two interesting facts that you have learnt from information at the display table.
>
> Write a question for a friend where the answer can be found at the table.

Create a buzz about the display table by encouraging children to contribute to it.

In addition to items on the resource list at the start of this section, the surface display could consist of items brought in by the children, for example:

- an object belonging to an older family member that may be of historical interest such as a telephone, magazine, piece of jewellery, item of clothing, photograph from a holiday many years ago
- books from the public library/home linked to a unit
- interesting items from nature
- a personal item that is special.

Accompanying the items with a card explaining who brought the item to school and what it is will encourage others to take notice and to want to do the same. Questions with a specific focus can be included or pupils could include a typed explanation in their own words, for example:

'This is Ganesha, one of the Hindu gods. We believe that he removes obstacles and so I worship him the night before I have a test at school.' By Rikesh

Lily has brought in this typewriter that belongs to her Grandma. Do you know what it is used for? What do we have nowadays that is similar to this?

This key ring is special to Jodie because it has her favourite character on it, Hannah Montana, and her aunty sent it from America. Do you think that a 6 year old in Africa would have something like this? Why or why not?

Yusef found this on the beach in the Costa Almeria in Spain. What do you think it is? Use the Internet to find out exactly where this area is. Do you think you would like to visit?

Stick to one or two focal points at a time on the display surface.

Do not allow the display surface to become overcrowded. Too many items and children often fail to see. Create a theme and change every once in a while, for example:

Then and Now (linked to a unit of study)

Artefacts from the past

Artefacts from another country

Find out about . . . (insert country)

Find out about . . . (insert period of history)

Find out about . . . (insert religion)

Surface display could focus around the questions, *How do we know? How can we find out about . . .?*

These questions, placed on a card, can be used to prompt pupils' thinking and can be asked of any area of study. For example:

How can we find out about life in Tudor times?

How can we find out about rivers in India?

How do we know about Mahatma Gandhi?

How do we know what is happening in other countries today?

The above types of questions encourage pupils to do more than just 'look' at the things on display, so instead of glancing at a map, for example, pupils begin to wonder how they can investigate rivers using the map. If, for example, sources of information related to an earthquake in Asia have been put out, such as newspaper articles, photographs, a previous weather report, first-hand accounts, etc., pupils consider 'How do we know about things that are happening elsewhere in the world?' This will bring to their awareness different types of media that exist and are available to us today as well as what we can find out from these.

PART 3

Finishing the job

Chapter 7

FOSTERING MULTIPLE INTELLIGENCES

As I said early on in this guide, this book is not just about setting up areas that look pretty, it's about developing a creative learning environment that encourages creative thinking. The most successful and inspiring way I have found of doing this is through implementing the 'Smart Wheel' – a set of activities that develop multiple intelligences. This, coupled with a straightforward management system that gives pupils responsibility for their own learning, provides a great opportunity to help you as a teacher bridge the gap between the more formal elements of your teaching and creative teaching.

I picked up the use of the Smart Wheel from a good friend and colleague some years ago and have used it avidly ever since. It was the first innovative teaching practice I came across that I felt I could incorporate easily into what I was already doing and could be carried out as and when it suited me. It put me on the right track to the more creative teaching approach that I had been striving for, helping my pupils to engage in creative thinking.

Since the day I set up my first classroom, I aimed for an environment that fostered creativity and independence in children. For years, my classroom consisted of a working class library and defined display areas. The display areas were connected to display tables for children to visit, where they could look at artefacts or resources, read information and take equipment needed for their work. There might also be the occasional extension activity for them to take to their desks to complete. Even though I had good control of the class, I was nervous about letting them loose on areas during lessons. Enticing, interactive display and resources were set up around the room, but when children would come up and ask if they could go and look at the science area for example, or play a game from the maths area with a friend, I would find myself answering, 'No, not now'. I felt that I should generally be facilitating more creative learning but the truth was that I just didn't have a clear enough idea of how I would organise and manage this. There didn't seem to be enough activities at the areas for every child to be engaged. Also, I felt that there was never time to allow children this free choice when we were always so busy with class work. I anticipated that there would be too much involved in creating more activities for the areas. So, needless to say, my room *looked* impressive, but was not being utilised to its full potential.

My colleague Anna had a similar classroom set-up to mine, but at times I would walk into her room and be in awe of the buzzing, productive atmosphere; children working calmly but not stifled; a mixture of groups and individuals; some working at their desks, some in other areas of the room. The lasting impression was that children appeared incredibly independent and were obviously enjoying what they were doing. Anna explained that for her, Smart Wheel activities were a successful addition to class work, catering for different styles of learning and automatically cross-curricular. It sounded perfect! She admitted that there was some work involved in getting the system up and running, but after that, it did not feel like a hassle at all and was easy to organise. She even let me into the secret that this could be a saviour, especially on those days when she needed the class to work independently because she felt under the weather or heaven forbid was less prepared than usual. She could rest assured that the children would still be engaged in purposeful, relevant activity.

So what is the Smart Wheel?

The Smart Wheel aims to accommodate and develop children's multiple intelligences. Mike Fleetham gives a clear, easy to read account of this in his book, *Multiple Intelligences Pocket Pal* (Network Continuum, 2007). Also, visit his website www.thinkingclassroom.co.uk for a quick reminder and an insightful questionnaire that can be used with pupils.

The wheel consists of 7 activities, each one tailored to a different intelligence:

- verbal–linguistic (word smart)
- logical–mathematical (logic smart)
- interpersonal (self smart)
- intrapersonal (people smart)
- bodily–kinaesthetic (body smart)
- visual–spatial (art smart)
- musical–rhythmic (music smart)

It all sounds impressive and so might appear complicated, but activities are quick and easy to come up with because key phrases provide a simple framework. By asking pupils to 'write . . .', 'create . . .', 'explain . . .', 'calculate . . .', 'demonstrate . . .' or 'play . . .' for example, many learning styles are accommodated.

How does it work?

The wheel (photocopiable template on page 81) is divided into seven sections with a pupil-friendly symbol on each to represent the seven multiple intelligences. Activities are then written in the appropriate section. Laminating the card makes it perfect for dry-wipe marker; activities can then be easily wiped off and changed. Alternatively, the wheel can be photocopied as needed. I like to enlarge the wheel to approximately A3 size. This way, it can be seen easily by pupils.

Four good reasons to embrace the Smart Wheel:

1   The wheel can take the focus of any curriculum subject, automatically exploring many cross-curricular elements. It provides an opportunity for an exciting range of activities that pupils ordinarily might not get chance to do.
2   Activities are likely to involve independent use of all learning areas of the room.
3   Having set up learning areas, you already have tailor-made activities for the wheel; you just have to identify which intelligence each activity fosters and then use them to make up the wheel.
4   Wheel activities do not have to be changed all that often. It will take pupils some time to complete all seven.

Please turn to pages 80–81 for the 'Multiple intelligences: a brief reminder' section and the blank photocopiable template of the Smart Wheel.

Pages 82–87 provide example Smart Wheels for literacy, maths, science, history, geography and R.E. for key stages 1 and 2. I have provided example activities that cater for different learning styles for these subjects. The starters, which are highlighted, can be used for numerous activities. On pages 92–98, you will find lists of more options for starter phrases, so play around with the wheel and enjoy!

Multiple intelligences: a brief reminder

 ## *Verbal-linguistic (word smart)*

Pupils enjoy oral discussion and the written word. They enjoy reading, creative writing, poetry, humour and impromptu speaking.

 ## *Logical-mathematical (logic smart)*

Pupils are very logical in their thought. They enjoy problem solving, puzzles, diagrams, sequencing and questioning.

 ## *Interpersonal (self smart)*

Pupils enjoy working on their own and are reflective in their thought. They enjoy goal setting and are able to understand and acknowledge their own strengths and weaknesses.

 ## *Intrapersonal (people smart)*

Pupils enjoy working in a group and are often strong leaders. They relate well to others and like to listen as well as lead. They enjoy paired work and peer tutoring.

 ## *Bodily-kinaesthetic (body smart)*

Pupils enjoy learning through movement using their gross motor skills and they like to fiddle with things. They enjoy role-playing, co-operative learning and field trips.

 ## *Visual-spatial (art smart)*

Pupils enjoy publishing their work, creating posters and art. They enjoy designing and structural based activities.

 ## *Musical-rhythmic (music smart)*

Pupils enjoy rhythm and beat, dancing, singing and humming along to musical performances.

Smark Wheel template

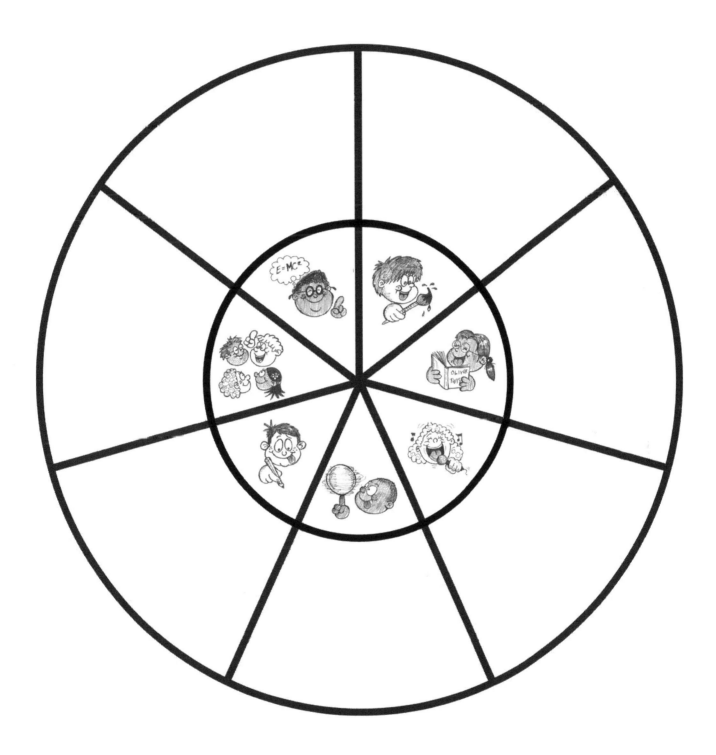

Literacy Smart Wheel activities

These activities could be used in any of the English areas in the classroom. The starters, which are highlighted, can be used for numerous activities.

Key stage 1

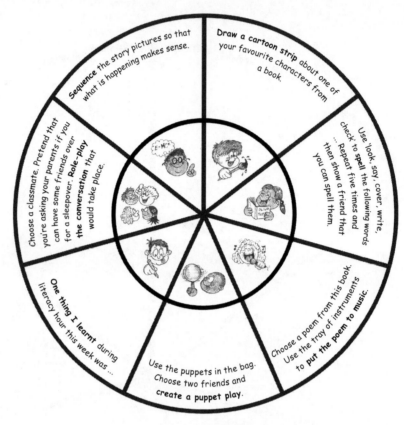

Key stage 2

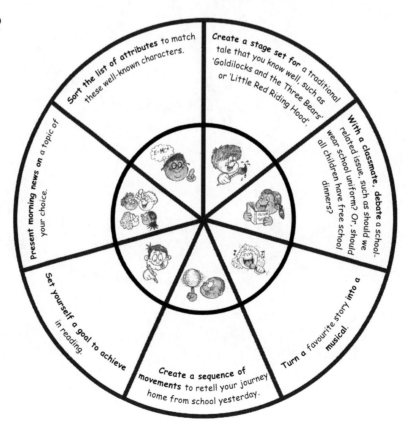

Maths Smart Wheel activities

Key stage 1

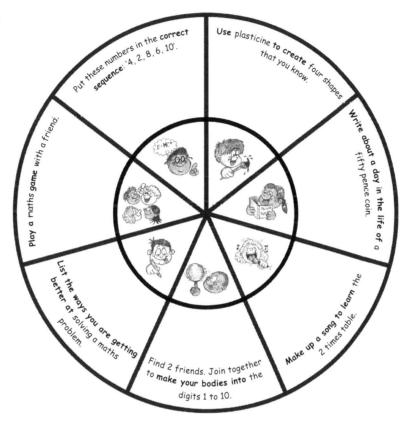

Key stage 2

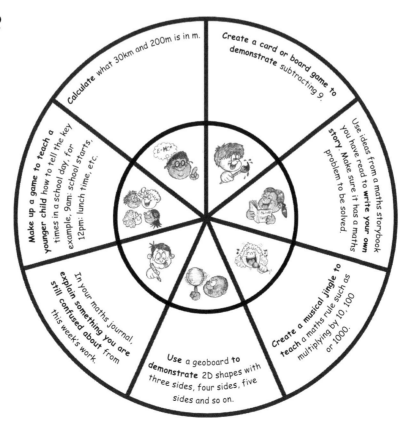

Science Smart Wheel activities

Key stage 1

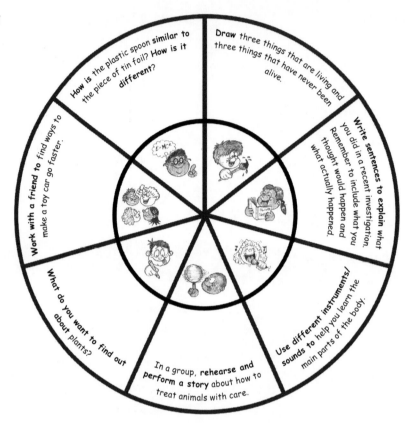

Key stage 2

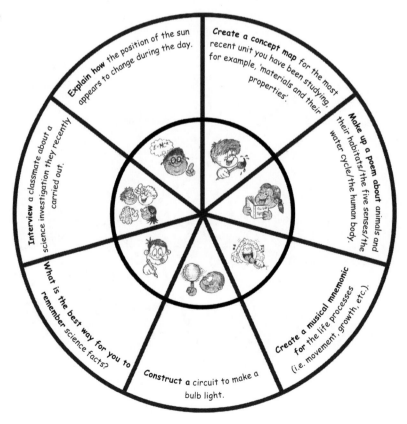

History Smart Wheel activities

Key stage 1

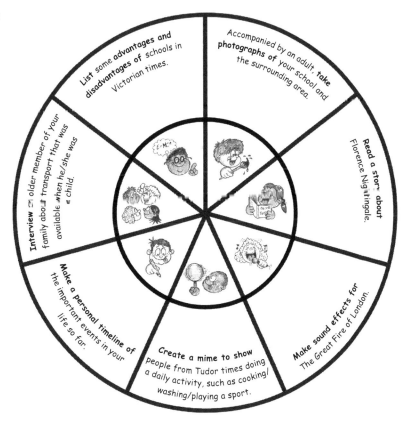

List some **advantages and disadvantages of** schools in Victorian times.

Accompanied by an adult, **take photographs of** your school and the surrounding area.

Read a story about Florence Nightingale.

Interview an older member of your family about transport that was available when he/she was a child.

Make a personal timeline of the important events in your life so far.

Create a mime to show people from Tudor times doing a daily activity, such as cooking/washing/playing a sport.

Make sound effects for The Great Fire of London.

Key stage 2

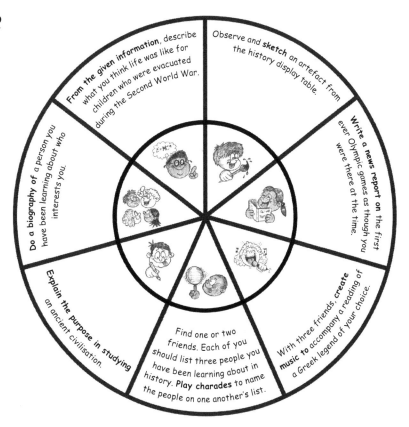

From the given information, describe what you think life was like for children who were evacuated during the Second World War.

Observe and **sketch** an artefact from the history display table.

Write a news report on the first ever Olympic games as though you were there at the time.

Do a biography of a person you have been learning about who interests you.

Explain the purpose in studying an ancient civilisation.

Find one or two friends. Each of you should list three people you have been learning about in history. **Play charades** to name the people on one another's list.

With three friends, **create music to** accompany a reading of a Greek legend of your choice.

Geography Smart Wheel activities

Key stage 1

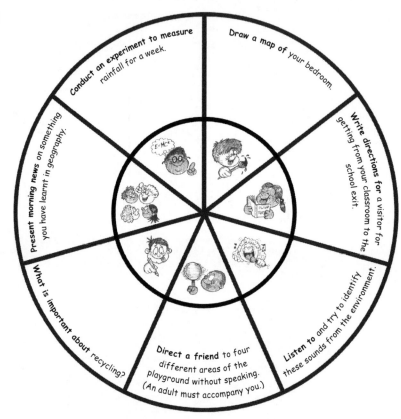

Key stage 2

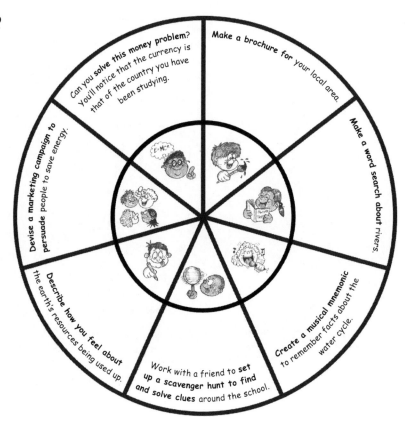

R.E. Smart Wheel activities

Key stage 1

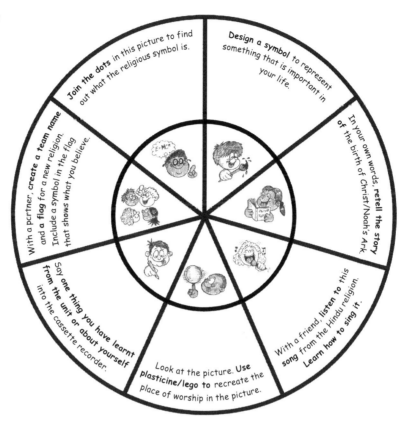

Key stage 2

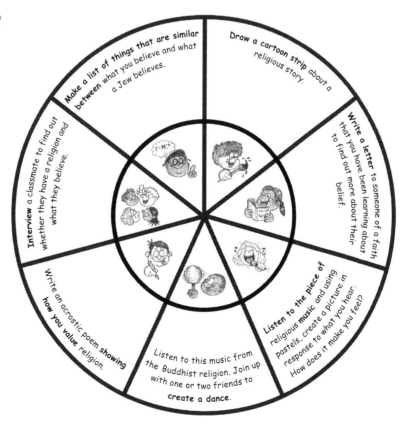

How do I prep my class for the Smart Wheel?

Your pupils will need some understanding of what the intelligences are; that each individual has a strength in a particular way that they learn. Help children see that the wheel offers a variety of experiences and therefore a variety of ways to learn. It will speak to each of their strengths but will also help them strengthen their weaknesses. A certain work ethic must be developed so that children use their time effectively. Below are some important aspects to decide on or discuss with your class.

Will your pupils need explanation of activities each time the wheel is changed?

This will depend on factors such as the age of your children and whether or not they are used to working independently. Time spent giving explanations, modelling and answering initial questions should get less and less as children become more familiar with this way of working and the types of activities they will encounter.

How long will children be given to complete activities?

This is completely flexible depending on what works for you and your children. Activities could be changed weekly, fortnightly or perhaps monthly. 'Smart Wheel time' may take place however often it works for you in your timetable; perhaps that is once a day, one afternoon a week or for two hours a week.

Do children have to work through every activity on the wheel?

Your pupils' individual needs will be taken into consideration here. During a week's worth of Smart Wheel time, some children may complete all seven activities, others only two or three. You will need to decide whether to set whole-class or individual targets for this.

Each time the wheel activities are changed, is it okay for pupils to begin with whichever activity they like?

Because individuals usually have a particular strength, they will no doubt be drawn to what they enjoy or find easy first. Will you establish a rule that states children must begin with a different 'smart' each time?

What do children do if they choose an activity and then discover that the necessary resources are already being used?

Should they simply choose another activity? Consider a signing-up system for certain equipment/resources such as computers, cassette/CD players or choose by writing children's names on lollipop sticks and drawing randomly.

Where will children record written activities?

For example, if working on the maths problem of the week, do children record their work? If so, do they record in their maths log, on a mini-whiteboard or on a piece of paper?

Where will children carry out the activity?

Are they allowed to work at one of the learning areas or should they take equipment to their desks? Can they work at a space on the floor? If it involves movement, is there a preferable place for this?

What do children do if they are 'stuck'?

Make them aware of the resources that are available at the learning areas to help them such as checklists, the word wall, writing prompts, reference books, maths aids and 'reminder' posters.

What is the expectation in terms of quality of work?

Is a certain standard of work to be expected? Will you accept work that has been rushed or is not the child's best effort? If an activity results in a performance or presentation, will there be a time to show/share?

How will I know that learning is taking place?

It is hard not to worry about 'proving' your children are learning. Assessment evidence you are required to provide will of course depend on your school's individual requirements, but there are some easy to implement techniques that you can carry out to help you recognise that learning is taking place.

Just remember to be clear about what it is you want to know the children have gained from a particular activity. Is it that they have shown understanding of a concept or skill taught previously? Perhaps it is the child's experience of using a particular intelligence that is of interest to you? Maybe you want to assess how well the child worked independently or in a group?

Be certain that the activities you include on the wheel are at an appropriate level for all of the children in your class. You may need to differentiate by setting individuals varying targets as to the amount of activities on the wheel you expect them to carry out or you may need to provide different wheel activities altogether for some children. If I can avoid the latter, I do, not because I am a lazy teacher, but because I believe that the wheel is meant to be inclusive, giving each child an opportunity to try. It's about building self-confidence, not destroying it. My solution is to provide activities that are open-ended and that are differentiated by outcome, enabling children to explore their capabilities.

Easy to manage assessment ideas

1   Snap photographs of the children whilst working and then annotate them with personal reflections of the experience or explanations of what they were doing. For example, 'Connor is using his bodily-kinaesthetic intelligence to. . . .' Follow with a quote from Connor of whether he enjoyed the task/found it challenging, etc.

2   Allowing children to share their work provides a useful opportunity to assess skills such as speaking and listening. If children are preparing a performance, let them know if what you are looking for is that they use a clear voice and address the audience.

3   Set aside 10 minutes towards the end of Smart Wheel time to ask pupils at random, 'What have you learnt today?' Pulling lollipop sticks with children's names on them out of a box is a good method of random selection and keeps children on their toes.

4   One way to record the development of pupils' social skills is to provide them with a sheet where they tick an option that applies to their current activity, for example, 'I am . . . working independently/interacting with someone else/working as part of a group.'

Keeping track

When there is a Smart Wheel on the go, you need some way of keeping track and making sure your pupils are experiencing all of the learning styles. Page 91 shows a few examples of simple, easy to produce recording sheets, suitable for different age groups for helping you and your pupils keep track of the completed wheel activities.

When should my class use the Smart Wheel?

The curriculum is jam-packed; the literacy and numeracy hour no doubt take up roughly 10 teaching hours a week, so I'm sure the question of 'When on earth do I fit this in?' still prevails.

Shayna, Year 6

Once my class got used to this independent way of working, I started to integrate the wheel into both numeracy and literacy hours, using it two sessions a week, usually Thursday and Friday. Because the objectives for the week have already been set, it only takes me about 20 minutes during my planning time to come up with something for each wheel activity that ties in and explores the relevant objectives.

Nicola, Year 1

Having taught the Foundation Stage for years using an integrated day approach and 'carousel', the Smart Wheel was easy to implement. Sometimes it's surprising how capable key stage 1 children are of working independently once they know the 'set-up'.

Raj, Year 4

My class and I love Smart Wheel time during history once we are into the swing of our topic. I used to feel that it was a real challenge to think of ways to vary up my lessons. The wheel makes this easy and I only need to change it about once a month.

Keeping track, figure 1

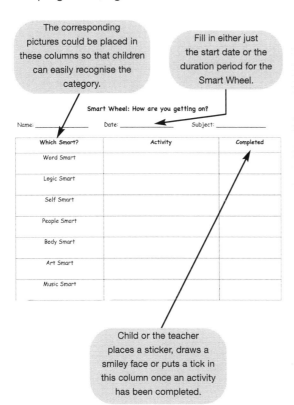

The corresponding pictures could be placed in these columns so that children can easily recognise the category.

Fill in either just the start date or the duration period for the Smart Wheel.

Child or the teacher places a sticker, draws a smiley face or puts a tick in this column once an activity has been completed.

Keeping track, figure 2

A picture works well for science or humanities subjects, as it can be unit-related. This will be appealing to pupils.

Once an activity has been completed, pupils colour the corresponding petal.

Pupils place a sticker or colour the appropriate square on completion of an activity.

Keeping track, figure 3

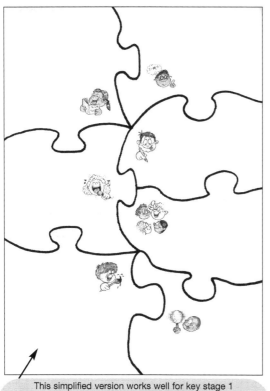

This simplified version works well for key stage 1 pupils because it isn't overwhelming. Pupil's name, date and subject can be written on the back of the sheet.

Children colour the appropriate jigsaw piece on completion of an activity.

Keeping track, figure 4

Smart Wheel : Maths

How is everyone getting on?

Name	Activity completed					
Sacha						
Kavita						
Keisha						
Thomas						
Jack						
Ben D.						

Produce this as a large chart for the wall. This provides an overview of completion of activities. This is a good option if you think your pupils might misplace an individual recording sheet. This type of chart may encourage some competition between pupils, so it's important to consider whether or not this is a good thing for your class of children.

The kids choose how they want to present what they have been doing and then towards the end of the month, we have two sharing sessions where they get the chance to share some of their work with the class. It has really helped with their skills at speaking in front of the class. Plus, a lot of the work they present can later contribute to wall display.

Bagwati, Year 3

In my classroom, the wheel sort of works like a 'Golden Time' that takes place every Friday afternoon. I tend to link the activities to current history, geography or R.E. topics. It takes the class about six weeks to work through them all.

Ambreen, Year 2

I enjoy using the Smart Wheel for science, even if it's just for one out of two of our weekly science lessons. It makes me feel that the children are really 'doing'. I like to not only include current unit work, but also revise past units through the wheel to help the children make connections.

Once the Smart Wheel is up and running:

- you will be confident that you're providing variety in your methods of teaching
- you will be able to link activities as and when you choose to curriculum learning objectives
- you will easily be able to incorporate many of the activities you already have set up at learning areas into the Smart Wheel
- you will see that your pupils are enjoying learning.

Word smart starter phrases

Use a dictionary to find the meaning of . . .

Retell the story of . . .

Write a letter to . . .

Write a caption for . . .

Write a story about the headline on . . .

Make a slogan for . . .

Narrate a story about . . .

Summarise a story/report about . . .

Create a crossword on . . .

Review a film/book/DVD about . . .

Define . . .

Read a story about . . .

Report on . . .

Write directions for . . .

Write a sequel/next episode to . . .

Create a limerick about . . .

Make up a riddle about . . .

Make a word search about . . .

Write a news report on . . .

Debate . . .

Study poetry about . . .

Spell . . .

Write a poem about . . .

Tell a story about . . .

Write about a day in the life of . . .

Logic smart starter phrases

Make a grid to show . . .

Explain why . . .

Make a code using . . .

Correctly sequence . . .

From given information, predict . . .

List the pros and cons of . . .

Calculate if . . .

Draw to scale . . .

Find the solution for . . .

Interpret research findings on . . .

Survey . . . about . . .

Estimate the probability of . . .

Devise equations for . . .

List reasons for . . .

Classify attributes of . . .

Hypothesise about . . .

Conduct an experiment in . . .

Analyse similarities in . . . and . . .

Find the pattern in . . .

Create number sequences in . . .

Compare . . . with . . .

Self smart starter phrases

What was most difficult about . . .?

Describe your experiences with . . .

What is the best way for you to remember . . .?

What do you want to achieve in . . .?

What do you want to find out about . . .?

You are good at . . .

What are your skills in . . .?

List the ways you are getting better at . . .?

Explain what you are still confused about/don't understand about . . .

One thing you need to concentrate on is . . .

One thing you learnt was . . .

What is important about . . .?

How does . . . relate to what you already know?

What helped you most to learn . . .?

Present your views on . . .

Describe qualities you possess that will help you to successfully complete . . .

Describe how you value . . .

Describe how you feel about . . .

Explain the purpose in studying . . .

Self-assess your work on . . .

Write a journal entry on . . .

Explain your personal philosophy on . . .

Set a goal(s) to accomplish . . .

How are you similar to . . . or different from . . .?

Identify your strengths in . . .

How could you be more . . .?

Choose which of these is most like you/least like you . . .

What did you do well/need to work on?

People smart starter phrases

In your group, reflect on . . .

Create a character to show . . .

Play a game with . . .

Devise a marketing campaign to persuade . . .

Mentor . . . on . . .

Negotiate with . . . about . . .

Present morning news on . . .

Do a biography of . . .

Conduct an advertising campaign to sell . . .

Collaborate with a classmate on . . .

Write a story or make up a game to teach a younger child to . . .

Practise the cooperative role of . . .

In your group, practise the cooperative skill of . . .

Conduct a class meeting to discuss . . .

Compare the following two people in terms of . . .

Carry out a survey in . . .

Work in pairs to . . .

Teach a classmate . . .

Tutor a younger pupil in . . .

Create a team slogan/banner/badge/logo/name for . . .

Work in a cooperative group on . . .

Work in a team to . . .

Role-play a conversation with . . .

Give a talk on someone who . . .

Research people who . . .

Interview . . . about . . .

Body smart starter phrases

Create a sequence of movements to show . . .

Make a human sculpture to show . . .

Use blocks/Lego/letters/a geoboard/cubes/tiles . . . to demonstrate . . .

Follow orienteering directions to . . .

Do a scavenger hunt to find . . .

Plan and go on an excursion to . . .

Choreograph a dance about . . .

Perform . . . to demonstrate . . .

Build or construct a . . .

Play ball games . . .

Cook and eat . . .

Identify body languages in . . . (cultures/gender/ages/status)

Play charades to . . .

Play a floor game about . . .

Rehearse and perform a story about . . .

Mime . . .

Create a dance . . .

Learn a dance . . .

Demonstrate body language to show . . .

Make your body into . . .

Act out the meaning of . . . (words/story/proverb/poem/play)

Take photographs of . . .

Make a video of . . .

Art smart starter phrases

Imagine and draw . . .

Make a brochure for . . .

Draw a cross-section of . . .

Use clay to create . . .

Draw a cartoon strip about . . .

Make a Venn diagram to compare . . .

Design a . . .

Draw a map/plan of . . .

Make a chart to show . . .

Design a stage set for . . .

Make a print of . . .

Draw a model of . . .

Create a diorama of . . .

Make an overhead transparency to teach . . .

Draw a map to show . . .

Take photographs to show . . .

Draw a flow-chart of . . .

Draw a concept map for . . .

Create a card or board game to demonstrate . . .

Compare graphics in . . .

Make a video/film about . . .

Imagine a bird's eye view of . . .

Visualise how to . . .

Devise a symbol/logo for . . .

Draw pictures/diagrams to show . . .

Music smart starter phrases

Use body or mouth percussion to express . . .

Create mood music for . . .

Move to this beat . . .

Make a soundscape for . . .

Listen for melody patterns in . . .

Create a musical mnemonic for . . .

Put something you have learnt to music

Make up a number rhyme/song about . . .

Play a rhythm game to learn . . . times tables/spelling words/rules, etc.

Create a rap song to teach . . . maths facts/grammar/spelling/rules/historical facts/definitions, etc.

Link different sounds to different feelings about . . .

Sing a song from . . . a period of history/a culture/a country/another language

Collect and present songs on . . .

Create a musical game to teach . . .

Write a new ending to a song so that it explains . . .

Find songs/music that express . . .

Provide musical accompaniment for . . .

Make/record music to show . . .

Make sound effects for . . .

Put a poem/story/play to music

Hum . . .

Turn the story of . . . into a musical

Draw/paint a piece of music as it plays

Listen to/list sounds from nature/the environment

Guess the instrument/melody/rhythm/song title/singer

Chapter 8

MAKING IT ALL WORK

The link between a creative classroom and effective learning

With each aspect of classroom set-up now complete or in the pipeline, you're ready to launch. But how do we make our room as appealing with children in it as it is without? The good news is setting up in the way I have described lends itself to good classroom management, enabling both the smooth running of your classroom and effective learning to take place.

Before letting them loose

The importance of learning routines

Before children start using areas of the classroom independently, I'm sure you don't need me to tell you that establishing class rules and behaviour expectations is key. None of what you are trying to achieve will be successful without the basis of solid learning routines. The challenge I always face is building up children's respect for the classroom long-term. No matter how much lecturing I do during the first few days of term about putting things back where they belong and taking care of books, etc., it doesn't take long before the majority of the class forget to keep caring.

Over the years, I have refined my approach to teaching children how to respect their classroom and use the areas within it effectively in line with 'The Responsive Classroom' technique, developed by *The Northeast Foundation for Children*. For more information, visit www.responsiveclassroom.org. Seeing this 'guided discovery' technique in action during visits to a New York state school convinced me to stop lecturing children about behaviour expectations and instead, guide them through a process in which they make their own discoveries about how to use and care for classroom materials; a technique that encourages enquiry and heightens interest. Dr. Belinda Gimbert (Teacher Educator from The Teachers.net Gazette) comments on the guided discovery technique: 'It offers teachers tools and techniques for creating a learning community that is nurturing, respectful and full of learning. It is possible to create a classroom that is enlivened by caring and respect, and such a classroom atmosphere is a critical foundation for learning ... We are building essential habits of self-control and care through the very routine of our classrooms' (*The Responsive Classroom: A Practical Approach for Teaching Children to Care*, Teachers.Net Gazette, October 2002).

A guided discovery approach to introducing learning areas

Introduce just one area at a time; make the starting point children's observations of what they first notice at that area – on the wall, on shelves, at the display table, etc. Begin with large items such as posters, signs and information on the wall; next, move on to items that are on display such as books, artefacts and activities, and then focus on resources that can be found in containers and drawers or cupboards. Record children's ideas and observations; some of these will be useful later when rules are generated and discussed. Discussion and questioning can be as simple or in-depth as is appropriate for your children.

Heightening awareness of what is on the wall

- Ask open-ended questions to find out what children notice and what knowledge they already have. For example:

  'What do you notice about these posters in the literacy area?'

  (Looking at a punctuation-reminder poster) 'Can anyone tell me something they already know about using capital letters and full stops?'

  'How might we use these posters to help us with our learning?'

  'Can you see any questions on this display board? What are they asking us to do/ think about?'

Exploring the items on display

- Direct children's attention to resources on display such as books, artefacts or activities and increase awareness by asking questions such as:

  'What are these things?'

  'Why do you think they are here?'

- If possible, gather children together on a carpet area or in a circle and either pass items around or allow children to look closely. Encourage an appreciation of resources by asking children to observe closely:

  'What do you notice about the . . .?'

  'What shapes/colours can you see?'

  'Is this new/old?'

  'Have you used . . . before?'

Knowing where to find resources

- Present children with scenarios of times when they might need certain resources, provoking them to think about how to approach a task independently:

  'If we're carrying out a science investigation, how will we know where to find what we're looking for?'

'How might these labels help us?'

'What will you do if you can't find something?'

Learning how to look after resources

- Generate ideas about how to care for the resources by asking:

  'What can we do to take care of the . . . when we use it?'

- Tell the children that you will watch carefully as they practise using a resource in the way the class has discussed. Observe them as they work, praising, reminding and redirecting if necessary.
- Gather children's ideas then ask one child to demonstrate:

  'Why is it important to put the . . . back where we found them?'

  'Can James show us a safe and careful way to take this equipment out and use it?'

  'Who was watching carefully? What did he do to show us how to use the . . . properly?'

Learning how to put things away

- Discuss why it is important to put things back where we found them and demonstrate how to do this.
  Ask a volunteer/s to demonstrate careful tidy-up:

  'Who can show us a safe and careful way to put away the . . .?

  'Everyone watch carefully to see how Keira handles the . . . as she puts it away. What did you notice?'

- Give opportunity for the whole class to tidy up. Support and praise pupils' efforts, reminding them of appropriate behaviour where necessary:

  'I'm going to watch as you put the . . . away safely.'

  'Well done blue table for listening so carefully.'

  'Remember to look at the label on the box to check you're putting the . . . back in the right place.'

Teacher tales

A Year 2 teacher, Sharmilla, tells of how she likes to play a trick on the class to help increase the 'bond' between the children and their classroom: 'When the class are out of the room, I mess up areas by knocking books over, emptying resources onto the floor and putting some resources in the wrong places. When the children return to the room, I make up a story I know they'll respond to (depending on their age) – perhaps the messy classroom elf did it or a mystery intruder? I then set the children the task of putting everything in order again. In my experience, this evokes quite a passionate response, causing children to want to take ownership of their classroom.'

Generating classroom rules

Carrying out a guided discovery process fully engages children, so when it comes to generating class rules, they will have a clear understanding of the purposes behind those rules, making them more meaningful.

- Pose questions that cause children to think about problems that might occur and how they can be handled, for example:

    'What if you need to use something that is already being used by someone else? What could you do?'

    'How many people do you think could be in the class library/at the writing area at one time? Why?'

    'Do you think it's fair to spend as long as you like at the computer?' 'Why/why not?'

- A similar use of questioning can be employed for devising class rules that encourage respect for one another in the classroom, for example:

    'How does it make us feel when one of our classmates doesn't share?'

    'Can we come up with a rule that is fair?'

    'What do you think is appropriate behaviour for when we're in the class library?'

- Record children's suggestions and explain that these will form our class rules/class contract that will be on permanent display in the classroom. By signing them, the children are agreeing to do their best to adhere to them at all times.

Following the guided discovery process in a way you see fit, will, without a doubt lead to children feeling motivated to explore and they will soon learn to make productive choices. Key points to remember in those all-important early days of term are:

- make sure children understand when they might use a resource and how
- involve children in demonstrations of the appropriate way to use an area of the classroom/classroom resources
- constantly reinforce the rules or contract developed as a class.

Classroom up-keep

Consider whether a 'monitor' system would work for you and your class. I find that having implemented the guided discovery technique for introducing learning areas, children then welcome the idea of class monitors/jobs to ensure that the classroom stays organised. Decide together on a list of possible jobs; then set up simple, short 'interviews' for the posts. If it is difficult to set time aside for this, ask children to write on a slip of paper why they think they would be good at the job of their choice, sign it and post it into a box for you to read later. If children think the selection of monitors is competitive and that they have to justify why they want a particular job, they are more likely to take it seriously. An alternative idea is to produce a rota whereby individuals, pairs or table groups take turns to be responsible for the organisation of an area of the classroom for a decided period of time. Whichever method you adopt, there must be a class understanding that ultimately, it is everyone's responsibility to respect and care for the classroom environment.

Posters and signs around the room help as constant reminders for pupils of how to look after and organise resources and how to conduct oneself in certain areas of the classroom. However, these signs can just as easily be ignored unless pupils' attention has been drawn to them from the beginning and they are referred to frequently. Consider making, or have children make, signs for the class library about looking after books; about procedures such as signing out and returning books and about 'Golden Rules' for certain areas such as the listening area or when working at a computer.

Up and running

Keeping control

We all have 'tricks of the trade' that we no doubt swear by for managing noise levels and behaviour conduct in the classroom. If you confidently want to allow children to use areas in the room independently, you have to feel that at any given moment, you can resume complete control of the whole class without shouting or fear of being ignored.

Popular methods include:

- Hand clapping to signal 'stop and listen'
- 'Copy me' patterns such as hands on head/shoulders/knees/nose that children copy to show they are paying attention
- Traffic lights displayed in the room:
  Red = silence and stop
  Amber = whisper/move quietly
  Green = use an 'inside' voice/move freely
- Turning the lights on and off to signal 'stop and listen'
- '1, 2, 3, freeze'
- Singing a chant or song that children join in with or understand to mean 'stop and listen' or 'return to your seat'
- Playing a piece of music which signals 'tidy up and return to your seat'

Teacher tales

'My most treasured resource for noise control is my "Noiseometer" that hangs all year round next to the whiteboard,' says Year 2 teacher, Manon. 'It looks like a large, card thermometer and has an arrow that can be moved up and down the scale. Sections are labelled from bottom to top as "whisper", "speak quietly", "speak normally" and "shout". We practise the appropriate voice for each level. Of course, children love to exercise their "shouting" voice, although it's rare that they get to use it! Children seem to enjoy looking to the noiseometer to see what it is set at for the activity. It makes my job easier because instead of repeating myself or raising my voice, I can simply point to the noiseometer as a reminder or ask the children to look and tell me what the noise level in the room should be.'

Encouraging positive behaviours

Superstar of the week

This is a favourite of mine that children always respond well to. It is awarded to one pupil each week, chosen by you, not for a specific achievement, instead to purely 'showcase' one individual a week (with of course, every child getting a turn). When announcing 'superstar of the week', create an element of surprise and suspense for the children, perhaps by playing special music (similar to a television awards show) and announcing into a pretend microphone or by closing your eyes and then pointing dramatically to the superstar or revealing a photograph of the selected pupil. The point is that it should be a big deal. The chosen pupil sits on special chair or cushion in the middle of the class circle. Go around the circle, inviting each child to say something positive about that person. This could highlight something they are good at or an admirable quality. Display the superstar's photograph surrounded by their classmates' comments on the classroom door outside until the next pupil's turn, when they take their 'tribute' home.

The 'WOW' work table

Something I remember seeing in a school I visited that left an impression was a table (alternatively, this could be a notice board) used to showcase children's work. The table was decorated with encouraging phrases such as *Well done*, *Congratulations*, *Number 1*, etc. and accompanying computer images. The teacher had hung four 'gold' medals above the table (found in a charity shop) that individuals could wear for the day if their work appeared on the table.

Wall of fame

I like to fill space along one side of my whiteboard with simple laminated commendations created on 'Publisher' saying,

> Literacy Whiz today is _____
>
> Maths Brainbox today is _____
>
> Science Boffin this week is _____
>
> Historical Hero this week is _____
>
> Class Geographer is _____

If the signs are laminated, it's easy to change children's names as often as you want and placing them at the front of the room means that they are visible to the class at all times.

A sense of belonging

I whole-heartedly believe that in addition to implementing the guided discovery technique and some sort of positive reward system, the final critical link for helping nurture children's

Teacher tales

'A big part of my classroom management strategy', says Lakshana, a Year 6 teacher, 'comes from "Class Awards". My class sit in groups of six and they are responsible for giving their table group a name based around an agreed theme. I then devise a behavioural reward system that allows the groups to earn points throughout the week towards gaining a special "award" for achievements such as "working sensibly", "cooperating with others", "packing away efficiently" or "lining up quickly". At the end of the week, points are totalled and a two minute "ceremony" is held, (accompanied by a class drum roll!) to hand out the awards that have been earned. The award is then displayed on the group's table for a few days until it is given back for another round of awards. The award is nothing more than a teacher-made trophy – a small, decorated piece of card, which on the back lists receivers of the award in chronological order and it stands on a tall photograph clip stand. It always surprises me that the children think it's so great. It's amazing how cooperative the class can be because they want to earn an award for their group.'

respect for one another, themselves, as well as for the classroom they spend the majority of their week in, is to invest time and effort into helping children feel that they belong and that each individual has an important part to play in making things work. It's essential that this groundwork be carried out early in the school year.

The following simple and perhaps familiar ideas aim to serve to inspire your own. They all make for eye-catching displays that work well in the early days of a new term; the point being that they involve the children in a way that helps them to bond as a class within their new surroundings and make them feel that their contribution is valued.

What's in a name?

Before the school year begins, I like to attractively display children's names on the door accompanied by a 'welcome' sign. This is such a simple step that immediately helps each child to feel part of the class community. Or, children create their own names for display and then later add to them with photographs and personal profiles. Another idea is for children to create name cards. I often tape these above children's pegs in the cloakroom or on children's desks. The activity can be made more meaningful by giving the task whereby the overall design of the name card must tell something about the individual. For example, each letter of a child's name drawn on piano keys tells that they like to play the piano.

Team builders

In the first week, I get the children to create a class jigsaw that follows a brainstorm about what it means to be a member of a team. I provide each individual/pair/group with a jigsaw cutout. On it they must express through words or pictures what they believe it means to be a member of a team. For example, sharing, listening to one another, letting everyone have a turn, etc. The pieces can be coloured or decorated and then put together to create either a picture or a pattern. This makes an attractive display with a title such as: *Class 3 – Piece by Piece*. I've also used 'bricks' instead of a jigsaw design to build up a wall, accompanied with a title like: *Building Class 2 – Brick by Brick*.

Making a mark

Create a bold and attractive mural of children's hand and footprints using paint. For a less messy option, trace around children's hands and feet and then cut out and decorate. I have used this to decorate a high-up wall display at the start of term to ease the pressure of filling the space with a topic-linked display.

All about us

A SPARK OF GENIUS   On a cut out flame, have each child write or draw something special about him/herself. This could reflect an aspect of their character, an interest or something they believe they are good at.

ME TIME   Children create individual multi-media collages depicting interests and personal information by cutting words and pictures out of magazines/catalogues or printing images and words from the computer. I have used these to create an *All About Us* class book that hangs in the class library.

ALL TOGETHER NOW   Have the class come up with a class motto that envelops what they want to be the ethos of their classroom. Alternatively, have each child contribute to a 'quilt' of class rules. It doesn't have to be made out of material; card can also look effective. I have displayed this in an unused communal area of the school – it stayed there for the duration of the school year.

FAMILY MATTERS   Each child creates a family shield to depict aspects of their family that are unique or important to them which they then share with the rest of the class.

Chapter 9

THE WOW FACTOR

At this point, there isn't much more to mention, yet I have saved my favourite element of classroom set-up until last – looking for opportunities to go the extra mile to make your creative classroom a *really* creative classroom. For me, adding all of the little extras is the most enjoyable – the bit to get excited about. We spend so much time in our classrooms; I have to *want* to be in mine and enjoy my surroundings. Creating the 'wow factor' is your chance to use your imagination as much as you want – have fun!

Create a 'wish list'

In addition to the homemade storage containers talked about in Chapter 3, there are items you may no longer have use for at home that can be used to add special touches to your room or for creative projects.

Waste not, want not

- rugs
- carpet tiles
- lamps
- large pieces of material
- clothes/hats/shoes
- plants
- paper cups/plates/plastic utensils
- large pieces of cardboard from boxes
- A4 sized card from cereal boxes
- printer paper used only on one side
- posters
- calendars
- fridge magnets
- picture frames
- books
- coasters
- buttons

Send out your wish list to parents. Some parents may have useful contacts through their work. Also, send it to local companies or factories to ask for a donation of supplies or that they consider you when throwing things out. Find out if your borough offers a 'scrap bank' for teachers where you can help yourself to card off-cuts, etc. Consider signing up to local recycling groups such as Freecycle.

Inject your personality

It's important to add touches of your personality to your classroom. Every teacher is very much an individual and if each of us reflects parts of our personal interest in the classroom (where appropriate of course), the children we teach will gain a rich and varied education as they journey through the school. Guaranteed to spark an interest, pupils will no doubt be inspired to share their own passions and interests with the class.

If you enjoy travelling . . .

Collect postcards or photographs from places you visit, encouraging pupils to do the same.

- Display the photos and postcards casually, perhaps on a notice board near your desk to create a 'Photo Wall': *Where have we visited?* Encourage pupils to include a brief written explanation of the picture or a question to accompany it.
- Display the pictures around the outside of a world map under the heading *Where in the world?* with arrows pointing to the country of the postcard.
- Make a 'Class Holiday Book' or 'Class Passport' where the postcards and photos are put in during a morning meeting or when there are 5 minutes to spare with a written caption and the children can go back and read this book at their leisure.

From your travels, bring back an artefact typical of the culture or country to put on display. Obviously, there has to be a limit to how much time you spend thinking about school when away from it (as my husband always says) but look out for items of interest that are free or inexpensive and don't take up a lot of room in the suitcase. It's always interesting to compare the language and layout of food and drink packaging to see how they reflect a culture or society. Don't bring anything in that is too special or precious to you, or if you do, make children aware of this and that you've decided to share it with them because you know they will be respectful. Again, children might like to do the same sort of thing.

If you enjoy art . . .

Display prints of famous artists' work with thought-provoking questions attached:

> Have you seen this painting before? Do you know who the artist is?
>
> This is called abstract art. What do you think this painting represents?
>
> (Painting of a water scene, for example) Imagine the sounds you would hear.
>
> (Painting of a subject, for example) What do you think the man in the painting is doing/ thinking?

Collect postcards of artists' work from museums. These make an interesting border across the wall.

Teacher tales

'When I first set up my classroom I felt like a bit of a fraud,' says Billy, a Year 4 teacher. 'I have a passion for old film posters. When everyone around me was setting up walls devoted to punctuation reminder posters and times tables charts, I filled spare bits of the wall with my treasured film posters. My justification was that they would cheer me up on a miserable day and would expose the children to something different. I realised that it probably wasn't very educational for me to stick them up without explanations, so I stuck cards to them with either information about film directors, actors or art styles used for the posters. Sometimes I attached questions that probed the kids to find something out. You could probably say I developed a rare breed of Year 4s who knew who Audrey Hepburn and Humphrey Bogart were!'

If you have an appreciation for music . . .

Expose your class to a variety of music at any opportunity.

If music calms you and puts you in a better mood, it will probably have the same effect on your class.

- Play music as pupils enter the classroom in the morning. Put a question for thought on the whiteboard for them to consider while listening, for example, *Have you heard this type of music before? Do you like it? What does it make you think of?*

- Play music at times when you want to create a certain mood, for example play relaxing music during an art lesson or lively music for a few minutes at a time of day when you want to perk the children up.

Class library: a little extra

Add soft furnishings to your class library to make it cosy and inviting. An armchair and floor cushions or a beanbag make a class library look like the perfect place to relax and read. Even if the area is already carpeted, a rug adds an extra touch of homeliness. A lamp in a class library looks homely and is calming. Check your school's health and safety policy though – I've known some schools that allow it and some that don't.

A colleague of mine once had a hammock strung across the corner of the class library – in it were an array of colourful cushions. Health and safety policy stipulated that the hammock couldn't be sat in, but the children were none-the-less excited by it and were allowed to take a cushion from it to sit on in the class library.

Your class library could take on a theme, perhaps voted for by the children. It doesn't have to be linked to a unit of work; it can be randomly chosen, just for fun. If your class library is already established or busy and you don't want to change it by adding a theme, you could create an additional small, themed area in the room for reading (if you have a large classroom). Here are some ideas:

- **The Reading Garden – *Grow with Books, Budding Readers***
  Include real or artificial plants, bright flowers made out of card/tissue paper, a cardboard fence, green rug to look like grass, butterflies hanging on string from the ceiling, a tree going up the wall which is then used for a specific class library focus, for example *The Reading Tree* with a leaf for each child holding a record of the books they have read.

- **A Jungle/Forest – *We're Wild about Books***
  Include animal print cushions/rug, animal soft toys, hanging vines, a tree, and long paper grass across the bottom of the wall.
- **An Ocean – *Reading is your Ocean, Fish Through Books, Dive into a Good Book***
  Include an ocean mural, a border of waves across the wall made from tissue paper (3D) or card, a mixture of blue and green crepe paper streamers hanging from the ceiling.
- **Outer Space – *Planet Reading, Visit the Astread Field, Float into Outer Space with a Good Book*.**
- **The Seaside – *Oh we do like to read beside the seaside, Explore our buckets of books*.**
  Include deck chairs and beach towels for children to sit on and sunglasses to wear whilst reading.
- **A bee hive – *Get Buzzy with Books, There's a Buzz about Books in . . . (class)***
- **A cave – *We're Batty about Books***
- **A tent – *Book Camp* (provide torches for reading)**
- **A wigwam – *Readwam***

Teacher tales

'I know it might sound bizarre', says Anna, a teacher of 11 years, originally from New Zealand, 'but I once had a bath in my class library! We were having our bathroom redone at home and instead of throwing it out, I decided to take it into school. I didn't regret it – I filled it with cushions and children were allowed to read in it, 3 at a time. I put up signs, "Bathe in Books" and "Soak up a Good Book". The children loved it.'

Aesthetically pleasing

Make display signs stand out

- Stand signs for a display table on photograph clip stands. IKEA sells fun-looking ones with a large coloured cube as a base, weighty enough to hold even an A4 sheet of paper.
- An old trick, but I still believe it makes for the effective display of items on a table – stand boxes/containers of different sizes on the table and then cover with a large piece of material. You may need to staple the material to the boxes in places to keep it intact. Items placed on the peaks and in the troughs will stand out and grab attention.
- Use chunks of polystyrene on a display board to stick signs on and make them appear 3D.
- Ripple signs to create a corrugated effect.

Plants make a classroom look cared for

Having plants in your room enables pupils to take responsibility for looking after them. Each table group could take charge of caring for a plant. Perhaps a local nursery/garden centre may be willing to donate.

Use material to add texture

Add texture to your room with something other than school backing paper. Visit a charity shop or market to look for interesting material that could be used to drape or cover tables/surfaces. Look for ethnic prints and material with patterns/prints/colours that link with a current topic. Connect the relevant display board and the table beneath by draping the material from the corner of the board to the table. If your display table can't be directly beneath the display board because of something else in the way, this is a good way of making sure that they are visually linked.

Hide what doesn't look pretty

Never allow the ugly back of a piece of furniture to show! If you want a bookcase or unit to jut out for example, perhaps create a sectioned off area, attach an attractive piece of wrapping paper, poster or material to the back of it. Similarly, freshen up a piece of shabby furniture by stapling material or backing/sugar paper to shelves.

Teacher tales

'I take every opportunity I can find to enhance my classroom with material', says Reception teacher, Louise. 'Some might say it's too much, but I think it creates such a homely feel and hides a multitude of sins. One year, my classroom was a Portakabin that sat at the edge of the playground. My pupils would be distracted when children were outside doing P.E. so I stapled some sheer turquoise material, gathered across the window to create a curtain effect. When the sun shone, a beautiful coloured light would be cast into the room.'

Show evidence of a multimedia-savvy classroom

In both the children's work on display and the signs, information and labels you place around the classroom, it is important to show the use of ICT. Remember to highlight how pupils have used ICT in their work process. Perhaps you could show/explain how they used the Internet to find information or display film stills or photographs (taken by you or the pupils) to give a sense of what pupils have been doing. Try to vary teacher-created display such as signs, labels, posters, etc., using a range of fonts and applications wherever possible.

Mounting work

Yes it's time consuming, but there are reasons why thoughtfully displayed work makes all the difference:

- For pupils, seeing their work displayed attractively gives them pride and adds value to the work they created.

- It's frustrating to look at work on display and not know the context or the process pupils followed in carrying it out.
- Questions for thought, along with clear titles and labels make the display more purposeful for children.
- The room looks so much nicer and shows the children that you're taking pride in their work.

If you're not already familiar with tricks of the trade that make pupils' work, titles, signs and labels pop, here are a few reminders.

The following sketches show the effects of varying thicknesses of mounts.

Quick cheat: a narrow inner border like this can be drawn with a thick, permanent marker pen to save time – a useful technique for mounting text that accompanies children's work on display such as information and explanations.

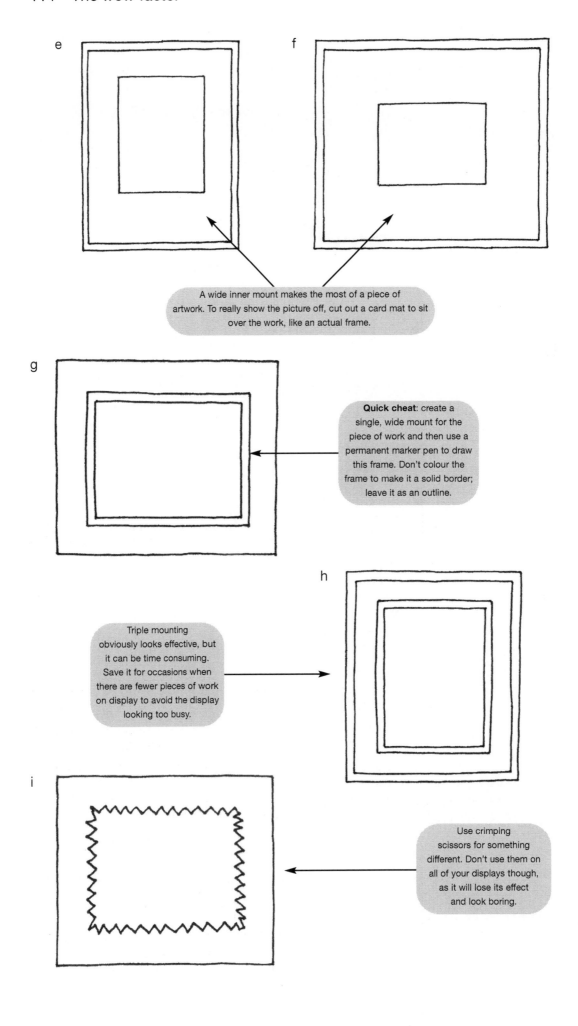

e

f

A wide inner mount makes the most of a piece of artwork. To really show the picture off, cut out a card mat to sit over the work, like an actual frame.

g

Quick cheat: create a single, wide mount for the piece of work and then use a permanent marker pen to draw this frame. Don't colour the frame to make it a solid border; leave it as an outline.

h

Triple mounting obviously looks effective, but it can be time consuming. Save it for occasions when there are fewer pieces of work on display to avoid the display looking too busy.

i

Use crimping scissors for something different. Don't use them on all of your displays though, as it will lose its effect and look boring.

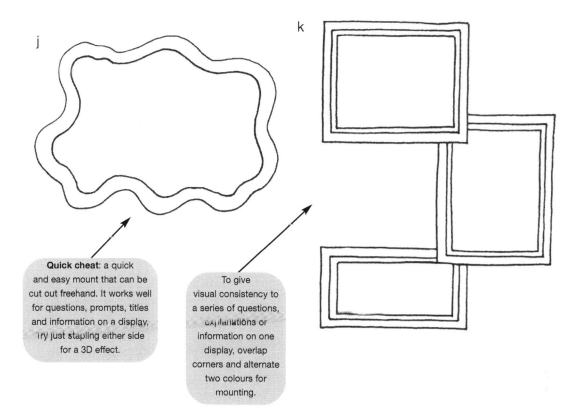

j

Quick cheat: a quick and easy mount that can be cut out freehand. It works well for questions, prompts, titles and information on a display. Try just stapling either side for a 3D effect.

k

To give visual consistency to a series of questions, explanations or information on one display, overlap corners and alternate two colours for mounting.

A note about colour

Here are a few guidelines to help you think about colour combinations that are interesting and pleasing to the eye:

- Place complementary colours next to each other – this makes each colour appear brighter. So for example, with primary colours:
  > red complements blue, yellow and green
  > blue complements red, yellow and orange
  > yellow complements red, blue and purple.
- Consider the effects of warm and cool colours. Reds, yellows and oranges are considered warm and blues and greens cool. Warm colours appear vivid and energetic; they can be used to make something 'pop', but you have to be careful they don't overwhelm the content of a display. Cool colours create a calming impression; they are less likely to overpower the content. Try using a single warm colour against a range of cool colours. So, try:
  > red against blues and blue-greens
  > orange against blues and blue-violets.
- If you want to play it safe, black as a final mount always appears finished and 'picture-framed'.
- Try variations in shade of a single colour. This will look clean and elegant and produce a soothing effect.
- Too many colours on one display can be tiring to the eyes and will detract from the work you are displaying. Three is a good number for colour, so for example, one colour for the backing paper to a display and two others for mounting the work.

Permanent display

If you have ideas up your sleeve for display that would remain relevant and worthwhile throughout the year, perhaps only needing to be altered slightly every once in a while, then go for it. It eases the pressure of feeling that all of your display boards need to be changed at the start of every term or half term.

 Add to the wow factor by making it visually apparent that each child is a valued member of the class community.

On black sugar paper/card create a portrait silhouette of each child. Use an overhead projector in order to outline each child's life size facial profile. The space inside the black silhouette can be used throughout the year for different things such as:

- children's self-reflections, 'How I feel about. . .' (work they have carried out)
- self-expressions, 'How I feel about. . .' (issues discussed in class such as bullying)
- class rules
- children's individual targets
- children's aspirations for the coming year.

 Devote space to a graffiti wall so that each child's voice can be heard.

All this involves is a piece of backing paper or cloth with lines drawn to look like bricks. It can be used for anything. Teacher questions regarding a topic of interest can be written on bricks to which pupils write responses or pupils can initiate their own philosophical thoughts or questions. It's a good way to cover 'citizenship' objectives or 'circle time' issues. Allow pupils to express their opinions before or following a class discussion on bullying, racism, current issues affecting society or common social dilemmas.

 Develop a culture of keeping up with current events among your children with a 'What's in the news?' board.

Invite the children to bring in newspaper clippings of interest and make a space for them on a wall/notice board or hanging in a plastic wallet (if space is limited). As this develops into a habit for the class, the children will enjoy and become more proficient at presenting their chosen articles and being involved in class discussion.

 Make your classroom visually multicultural through display.

If there is a language other than English spoken by a high proportion of children in your classroom, label items around the room in dual language.

Create a poster of *Languages we speak in . . .* (insert class name)

Make signs for areas such as *Art Area* with the translation in lots of different languages written around it.

Display a *Word of the week* using a different language each week. Challenge older children to find out what the language is and what the word means.

Capture pupils' and visitors' attention with an accent to highlight what the class is studying.

Make a big TV screen or window. It could be placed as a frame for a display board or if you make it out of a large cardboard box, it can stand 3D in front of the display board or hang from the ceiling with pupils' work attached behind it.

Ask: 'What's on TV this week?' or 'What can you see through the window?'

Create a made-up character to make a display more enticing to pupils.

Make a large character out of card. This could be a popular favourite character, a character from history, a scientist or an imaginary classmate for example. The character can appear to be posing the questions that are on display. For example:

> Help Suzy Scientist in her lab to decide which of the items are solids, which are liquids and which are gases by sorting them into the correct beaker.

> This Roman soldier wonders how life now differs from life in his day.

> Our new classmate Rory is super-brainy. Can you answer his questions?

'Build' a 'learning wall' to encourage children to self-reflect.

Devote a display board to a 'learning wall' on which children place 'bricks' to show something they have learnt. It could be unit content-linked or a personal achievement to do with behaviour or attitude.

Display a 'levels ladder' to help children self-assess.

Make a 'ladder' out of card and label each rung as a national curriculum level, ascending from least to most sophisticated. The range of levels you include will depend on whether you teach key stage 1 or key stage 2. Place level descriptors on separate, colourful card pieces between the rungs. For example, if creating a ladder for literacy, then surrounding *level 1*, include *I write simple words and phrases, I use full stops*, etc. On the opposite end of the ladder, *level 4* would include, *I use complex sentences, I choose adventurous words for effect*, etc. Accompany the ladder with the questions, *Which level are you working at? Set yourself a target. How will you up-level your next piece of writing?*

Filling hard to reach spaces

Whether or not hard to reach spaces are a concern for you will depend on the design of your school building. I have had to decorate many a classroom where there has been a display board placed ridiculously high on the wall or above the whiteboard.

- Look out for popular book posters or posters with children's film characters on them. Place a speech bubble next to one of the characters' mouths, saying something that sets an example or deals with a citizenship issue. For example, 'We work as a team to get things done.'

- Ask DVD rental stores, music stores or supermarkets if you can have the large cardboard characters used in promotions – these can be lots of fun and require no work from you, but automatically brighten up an area as well as inject interest.
- Place several clocks next to each other showing times around the world. This links geography, maths and science. Countries shown could be changed to tie in with units of work.

We want our classroom to be a place where children have a thirst to come and learn; a place that stretches children's imaginations and a place that others notice. Personally, what makes my efforts especially worthwhile is the enthusiasm children show when they first arrive in my classroom at the beginning of the school year and start noticing and taking in the things around the room that I have purposefully put in place to challenge, inspire and help them in their learning. Or, when my adding or changing something in the room at any time of the year causes a buzz. The children I teach always know how much I care about our classroom and this, without a doubt serves to increase their interest and their respect.

A final note: Do not let this guide sit on the shelf with a *Some good ideas if I ever have time* sticky note attached! If you don't follow the set-up process, please dip in to the activity ideas or vice versa. If I can inspire a fellow teacher to explore the freedom of creativity in the classroom or if I can help ease just some of the pain in the mammoth task of trying to set up a classroom that looks 5-years established and runs like a well-oiled machine, then I can return to my paint-cracked, furniture-challenged, sugar-papered home-from-home feeling contented.

16909714R00072

Printed in Great Britain
by Amazon